Barnabas
A good man, full of

People IN — THE BIBLE

Robert Dale

Day One

© Day One Publications 2007
First printed 2007

ISBN 978–1–84625–088–0

Unless otherwise indicated, Scripture quotations are from the **New King James
Version (NKJV)®**. Copyright © 1982 by Thomas Nelson, Inc. Used by permission.
All rights reserved.

British Library Cataloguing in Publication Data available

Published by Day One Publications
Ryelands Road, Leominster, HR6 8NZ
☎ 01568 613 740 FAX 01568 611 473
email—sales@dayone.co.uk
web site—www.dayone.co.uk
North American—e-mail—sales@dayonebookstore.com
North American—web site—www.dayonebookstore.com

Cover design by Wayne McMaster
Designed by Steve Devane and printed by Gutenberg Press, Malta

This is a very uplifting book. Here you will find copious investigation, studious exposition and judicious application from the biblical record of a generous man so full of Christ that he was a constant encouragement to the church. What more could you ask for?

—John Benton, pastor of Chertsey Street Baptist Church, Guildford, and editor of Evangelicals Now

It is easy to underestimate the apostle Barnabas, who is overshadowed by his fellow worker, the apostle Paul. Robert Dale's study displays Barnabas' godly character, increases our appreciation of his role in the growth of the New Testament church, and draws numerous insights of application for personal godliness and the work of the ministry. Recommended for pastors and lay readers.

—Les Bollinger, Pastor, Beaver Baptist Church, Beaver, Pennsylvania

Contents

If Christians were to vote for their favourite Bible character, Barnabas would surely be in the top ten. Most of us feel instinctively drawn to this warm-hearted disciple, who so wonderfully lives up to his name, 'Son of Encouragement'.

It is no accident that so many Christian organizations have used the name Barnabas. There is the Barnabas Fund, which encourages prayer and support for persecuted Christians; the Barnabas Trust; the Barnabas Hospice; and no doubt many others. My own son worked for two years for Barnabas Adventure, which runs adventure holidays for children—encouraging them to believe that they can climb that tower and paddle that kayak.

Encouragement is the common theme, and what an important theme it is!

Derek Wood's delightful book, *The Barnabas Factor—The Power of Encouragement* (IVP) is a 'must-read' on this subject, but I cannot find another book just about Barnabas. I hope that this book will help to fill that gap, and help readers to appreciate—and maybe imitate—this wonderful man, who himself is a reflection of a still greater Man, our Lord Jesus Christ, the greatest Encourager of all.

A generous gesture

Acts 4:36–37

The first thing we need to know about Barnabas is that Barnabas was not his real name! His real name was Joses (the Greek form of Joseph). 'Barnabas' was a nickname given to him by the apostles. The AV calls it a surname, 'Joseph Barnabas'.

Barnabas, we are told, means 'Son of Encouragement'. Literally, it means 'Son of Prophecy', but encouragement was one of the major functions of prophecy.

It is worth pausing at the outset to consider this name as Luke explains it. The Greek, *huios parakleseos* ('Son of Encouragement'), is related to the word *parakletos*, used by our Lord of the Holy Spirit in John 14:16: 'Helper' (NKJV), 'Comforter' (AV) or 'Counsellor' (NIV). Barnabas (like Stephen) was a man 'full of the Holy Spirit'.

The expression, 'Son of …' was a common one in Hebrew. James and John are called 'Sons of Thunder'; Paul calls Elymas, 'son of the devil'. The idea is simple: a son of something is someone filled with that quality—Barnabas therefore is full of encouragement.

It is not hard to see why the apostles gave him this name.

Even here, in this first encounter, we see Barnabas giving generously to those in need—what an encouragement that must have been to the early church!—both helping the poor and encouraging others to do likewise.

As the story goes on, we will see many more examples of Barnabas the Encourager—encouraging the newly converted Saul in Acts 9, encouraging the new church in Antioch in Acts 11, encouraging young John Mark in Acts 15. But more of that later.

For now, let us go back to the beginning.

An unknown past

Where did this man come from? Barnabas appears in Scripture quite suddenly in Acts 4—rather like Elijah the Tishbite suddenly bursting onto the scene in 1 Kings 17. All we are told about him is that he was a Levite from Cyprus, and that he had land to sell. Half a lifetime is bound up in those words! How much there is we would like to know, and how much we are left to guess!

Cyprus, as many modern tourists will know, is a beautiful island, sixty miles south-west of Antioch. It is called Kittim in the Old Testament. For the Jews it was their first landfall by sea, and many of the Jews of the Dispersion had settled there. Apart from all the usual Mediterranean fruits, Cyprus was famous for copper (hence the name). Many Jews worked in the mines, and the island had many synagogues.

As a Levite, Barnabas was not allowed to own land in Israel—but he could, and did, own land overseas; this presumably is what he sold.

As a Jew, he would have been taught the Scriptures from childhood—like Timothy, who 'from childhood' had 'known the Holy Scriptures, which are able to make you wise for salvation' (2 Timothy 3:15). He would also have attended the synagogue each Sabbath.

How old was he? There is no way of knowing. We imagine him, perhaps, as an older man; he seems like a father-figure to Paul.

What brought him to Jerusalem? We do not know. There is a tradition that he came, like Saul, to study—but there is no evidence. He could have come to fulfil his duties as a Levite—the Levites traditionally took care of the temple—though by now there were many more Levites than were needed. He might have come on a family visit. Colossians 4:10 mentions his 'cousin' Mark (AV says 'nephew'), whose mother Mary had a house in Jerusalem, where the church met for prayer (Acts 12:12).

Most likely, he was there, as a devoted Jew, for Pentecost. Acts 2:9–11 mentions Jews from all over the world gathered in Jerusalem—'Parthians and Medes and Elamites, those dwelling in Mesopotamia, Judea and Cappadocia, Pontus and Asia, Phrygia and Pamphylia, Egypt and the parts of Libya adjoining Cyrene, visitors from Rome, both Jews and proselytes, Cretans and Arabs'. Admittedly, Cypriots are not mentioned, but surely they were there, and maybe Barnabas was among them, staying, perhaps, with Mary.

An early convert

Which brings us to the question, When was he converted?

Strange to say, this is another unanswerable question. You might have expected that the New Testament would give us Barnabas' testimony. But actually, the New Testament is rather sparing with testimonies. We have Paul's testimony, but nothing for most of his fellow-workers.

That, perhaps, ought to make us pause and think.

We set great store by testimonies—how did a person come to Christ? A good testimony can be a great encouragement. But the New Testament is generally more interested in how you are *walking* with Christ than with how you *came* to Christ. The most wonderful testimony can turn out to be a false dawn, whereas the quietest and most uninteresting testimony can be the beginning of a wonderful Christian life.

Quite clearly, Barnabas was an early convert—but we have no means of knowing precisely how or when he came to faith.

There is a tradition, recorded by Clement of Alexandria in the late 2nd century (in his *Stromata, Book 2*), that Barnabas was one of the 'seventy' in Luke 10—but there is no independent evidence for this. He could have been converted on the Day of Pentecost, or at any time in the wonderful days that followed.

But the Bible does not say. It is enough that he was a believer. And that is all the Lord asks of us—not a story (good though that is), but faith. Barnabas had somehow come to trust in Christ as his Lord and Saviour—and now he showed his faith in this magnificent gesture, selling his land, and laying the money at the apostles' feet.

A golden age

These were golden days in the life of the church. After the outpouring of the Spirit in Acts 2, Peter had preached, and 3000 were converted. The life of the church is described in Acts 2:42–47:

They continued steadfastly in the apostles' doctrine and fellowship, in the breaking of bread, and in prayers. Then fear came upon every soul, and many wonders and signs were done through the apostles. Now all who believed were together, and had all things in common, and sold their possessions and goods, and divided them among all, as anyone had need. So continuing daily with one accord in the temple, and breaking bread from house to house, they ate their food with gladness and simplicity of heart, praising God and having favour with all the people. And the Lord added to the church daily those who were being saved.

Since then, persecution had broken out. The church had prayed, 'Lord, look on their threats, and grant to your servants that with all boldness they may speak your word, by stretching out your hand to heal, and that signs and wonders may be done through the name of your holy Servant Jesus' (4:29–30). And the Lord answered by shaking the whole house, and filling them afresh with the Spirit.

After this, we read of a church vibrant with the power of the Spirit:

The multitude of those who believed were of one heart and one soul; neither did anyone say that any of the things he possessed was his own, but they had all things in common. And with great power the apostles gave witness to the resurrection of the Lord Jesus. And great grace was upon them all. Nor was there anyone among them who lacked, for all who were possessors of lands or houses sold them, and brought the proceeds of the things that were sold, and laid them at the apostles' feet, and they distributed to each as anyone had need (4:32–35).

Enter Barnabas

It is against this background that Barnabas brought his gift: 'Joses, who was also named Barnabas by the apostles (which is translated Son of Encouragement), a Levite of the country of Cyprus, having land, sold it, and brought the money and laid it at the apostles' feet' (4:36–37).

This gift must have made a great impression. Here was a man doing what the rich young ruler in Luke 18 refused to do—giving up his riches for the sake of Christ.

Was it this gift that led the apostles to call him 'Barnabas'? Luke does not say so; he seems to imply that Barnabas was already known to the apostles. But this gift must have established his reputation, once and for all, as a man with a great heart, who would do anything for Christ—a man of love, who cared for the poor, and a man of God, whose treasure was in heaven, and who cared nothing for the things of this world.

[handwritten margin note: PROBABLY IT WOULD HAVE TAKEN A LOT MORE THAN THIS]

This gift stands in stark contrast to the sordid selfishness of Ananias and Sapphira in chapter 5, who sold land, and gave *part* of the proceeds—and lied about it. They were struck down dead, but Barnabas is raised up high. Their reputation is ruined (and they probably wanted a reputation for Godliness), whereas Barnabas' reputation (which he did not seek) is established.

SHARING OUR POSSESSIONS

Should Christians today imitate this sharing of property?

Most of the commentaries insist that this is not required of us, nor even particularly wise. Some call it 'an early experiment in communism'; others compare it with the common ownership of property in the monastic orders.

It is quite clear, however, that Luke reports all this with enthusiasm—perhaps even with nostalgia, writing many years later.

This was *not* an early experiment in communism. Communism is an atheistic philosophy, which elevates the state above the individual, and makes the pooling of resources compulsory. What happened in Jerusalem was voluntary.

Nor was it an early experiment in monasticism. Monasticism is a retreat from the world; these people continued their normal lives in the world. They were simply attempting to share what they had.

The biblical ideal is that every man should sit 'under his own fig tree and under his vine'—in other words, that each should have what he or she needs. Riches are recognized as a gift from God—but also as a responsibility. Paul writes in 1 Timothy 6:17, 'Command those who are rich in this present age not to be haughty, nor to trust in uncertain riches but in the living God, who gives us richly all things to enjoy.' Often we stop there, and rejoice in our riches, but Paul goes on—'Let them do good, that they be rich in good works, ready to give, willing to share, storing up for themselves a good foundation for the time to come, that they may lay hold on eternal life' (1 Timothy 6:18–19).

Barnabas and others were obeying that, before it was written!

TREASURES IN HEAVEN

Paul's teaching also suggests a further dimension. It is not only for the benefit of others that we should share, but also for ourselves! By sharing, we are laying up 'treasures in heaven'.

Barnabas and others were actually following our Lord's counsel to the rich young ruler, in Luke 18:22—'Sell all that you have and distribute to the poor, and you will have treasure in heaven; and come, follow me.'

That was our Lord's counsel to one man who was taken up with riches—and he refused to follow it. It is not a universal command. And yet it contains a universal principle—that we must serve God and not money, for 'No one can serve two masters' (Matthew 6:24).

SPIRITUAL LIBERATION

Perhaps also there was another benefit. Apart from helping the poor and investing in eternity, Barnabas was setting himself free from worldly concerns. He would no longer have to go back to Cyprus to manage his estate; he could concentrate more on spiritual work—very helpful for a future missionary.

How much of our time and energy is taken up with worldly concerns! How often the seed of God's Word is 'choked with cares, riches, and pleasures' (Luke 8:14)! Would a little sharing help?

The Bible does not encourage foolhardy gestures. We are not to impoverish ourselves in order to imitate Barnabas! But his generosity is an example to us.

Years ago, as a young Christian, I once spent an evening with a group of believers who were talking about sharing. Then one of them stood up, and put a £5 note on the mantelpiece. It had an electrifying effect!

How many Christians are 'heaping up riches' for themselves (Psalm 39:6)! Barnabas was not. His treasure was in heaven. Is yours?

A true friend

Acts 9:26–27

After bursting onto the scene in Acts 4, Barnabas disappears again for five chapters. He reappears in Acts 9 as the man who introduced Saul—later Paul—to the apostles, and gained acceptance for him in Jerusalem.

For this alone he deserves our gratitude.

Just imagine a few possible scenarios if Barnabas had not stepped in.

Suppose Saul had patiently approached every little group of Christians in Jerusalem and been rejected by them all: the apostles refuse to see him; Peter preaches against him as a 'wolf in sheep's clothing'; and finally a frustrated and embittered Saul gives up and forms his own rival church—or worse still, goes back to the Pharisees and denounces the church as a sham, preaching love and practising hate.

Or imagine the disciples in Damascus—who *had* welcomed him— hearing about the way Saul had been treated, and separating from the church in Jerusalem.

Think too, what the church would have lost without Paul—no letters, no missionary journeys! Barnabas was a vital link in the chain.

This episode also shows Barnabas in his true character as an encourager.

Barnabas the advocate

'Son of Encouragement', remember, is *huios parakleseos* in Greek. *Parakletos* means literally 'one who is called alongside'; it is translated 'advocate' in 1 John 2:1—'We have an Advocate with the Father, Jesus Christ the righteous'. The NIV translates it as 'one who speaks … in our defence'. Here, Barnabas is acting as Paul's advocate. He literally comes alongside him to speak in his defence; just as Christ is our advocate in heaven, so Barnabas was Paul's advocate in Jerusalem—a truly Christlike character!

But let us follow through the story in sequence.

A spiritual environment

Several years had passed since Barnabas had sold his land, and much had happened in that time.

Acts 5 records the terrible story of Ananias and Sapphira—the couple who lied about their gifts, and were instantly struck dead. Not surprisingly, 'great fear came upon all the church' (5:11).

But the church went from strength to strength. 'Through the hands of the apostles many signs and wonders were done among the people. And they were all with one accord in Solomon's Porch. Yet none of the rest dared join them, but the people esteemed them highly. And believers were increasingly added to the Lord, multitudes of both men and women' (5:12–14).

This was the spiritual atmosphere in which Barnabas had lived.

All of us, to some extent, are the product of our spiritual environment. In a time of revival, even the weakest believers are turned into prayer warriors, not only by the power of the Spirit within them, but also by the example of other believers around them. On the other hand, in times of spiritual dryness, young believers learn by example that worldliness is acceptable, occasional church attendance is sufficient, and only the minimum of effort is required for the Lord. We praise Barnabas for his spirituality, and rightly so—he was one of those who set an example—but he himself breathed-in this atmosphere of spirituality, which filled the early church.

We need to be aware of the influence of the spiritual environment, and, if necessary, rise above it. We need to be aware also of our own influence upon others, seeking always to set a good example. We should be able to say, with Paul, 'Imitate me, just as I also imitate Christ' (1 Corinthians 11:1).

Persecution

But opposition soon arose. It always does—wherever the Lord is at work, Satan is not far behind. The apostles were imprisoned by the Jewish authorities. What a shock this must have sent throughout the church!

But straightaway, the Lord delivered them: an angel opened the prison doors. They were arrested again, and commanded *not* to preach—but Peter replied, 'We ought to obey God rather than men' (5:29). The authorities were furious, but Gamaliel calmed them down, urging them not to act hastily, lest they be found fighting against God.

As far as we know, Barnabas took no part in these events, but presumably he was there, watching and praying, and learning to be bold.

After this, a fresh challenge arose. The increasing demands of poor relief required extra help and seven deacons were appointed—men 'full of the Holy Spirit and wisdom' (6:3). Barnabas might have made an excellent deacon, but he was not chosen: God had other plans for him. But he must have been learning from what he saw. In Acts 11, we find him doing the work of a deacon—bringing gifts for the poor from Antioch to Jerusalem.

Meanwhile, the church continued to grow—in 6:7, 'The number of the disciples multiplied greatly in Jerusalem, and a great many of the priests were obedient to the faith.' How Barnabas, as a Levite, must have rejoiced in that!

Saul appears on the scene

But then the storm broke. One of the deacons, Stephen, was also a mighty preacher, and incurred the wrath of the Synagogue of the Freedmen—possibly Saul's synagogue—and he was brought before the Sanhedrin. Acts 7 ends with Stephen being stoned, and, ominously, 'the witnesses laid down their clothes at the feet of a young man named Saul' (7:58).

This is the first time Saul has appeared, and, immediately, he takes centre stage as the arch-enemy of the Christians.

A particularly vicious persecution began: 'At that time a great persecution arose against the church which was at Jerusalem; and they were all scattered throughout the regions of Judea and Samaria, except the apostles ... As for Saul, he made havoc of the church, entering every house, and dragging off men and women, committing them to prison' (8:1,3). Presumably, Barnabas also left.

However, God had his hand on Saul, and in Acts 9 we read of his dramatic conversion on the road to Damascus. Saul, 'still breathing threats and murder against the disciples of the Lord' (v. 1), was heading for Damascus with authority from the high priest to arrest the Christians and bring them bound to Jerusalem. But the Lord arrested him instead! As he drew near to Damascus—the Lord loves to act at the eleventh hour!—he saw a great light, and heard a voice: 'Saul, Saul, why are you persecuting me?' (v. 4). It was, of course, the voice of Jesus. Blinded by the light, he was led into the city, and three days later,

Ananias came to heal him, baptize him (22:16), and to tell him his future mission. Immediately he began preaching.

People must have wondered, was this a genuine change of heart, or an elaborate trick? The church in Damascus, however, accepted him in good faith, and eventually the Jews also accepted that Saul really had changed sides—and they plotted to kill him. Saul had to be unceremoniously bundled out of the city—let down through the wall in a basket—and so he came to Jerusalem.

A challenge for the church

Now Saul (as he was still called) quite naturally tried to join with the disciples in Jerusalem. You may ask, 'What disciples?' Hadn't they all been scattered? But presumably some had returned, and the apostles, of course, were still there. Saul tried to join with this little flock in the Holy City—what an example to us to seek out fellowship wherever we go, and to join with the local church. It was a brave decision on Saul's part. After all that had happened, he would have some apologizing to do!

But the disciples in Jerusalem were not prepared to welcome him. 'They were all afraid of him, and did not believe that he was a disciple' (9:26).

Now this was understandable. This man had persecuted them; some of them perhaps could remember the knock on the door, or had lost loved ones. They only had his word for it that he was converted; surely, they would think, this man could *never* be converted. After all he had done, he was destined for judgement! This was surely a trick. He was trying to infiltrate the church, to find out who they were and where they lived. A wolf in sheep's clothing—but this frightened flock could see through it. This was a wolf waiting to devour them.

How frustrating it must have been for Saul! They had accepted him in Damascus—but then those believers had never experienced persecution from Saul. In Jerusalem they had, and they were understandably wary.

Enter Barnabas!

Barnabas *was* prepared to accept Saul. Here was a man with a loving heart, prepared (as Paul himself later put it) to 'bear all things, believe all things, hope all things, endure all things' (1 Corinthians 13:7). He could even dare to hope that Saul had been converted.

There is no indication that Barnabas had previously known Saul, other than by reputation. But he had listened to his story, and he was convinced.

What is more, he was prepared to take up Saul's cause in a practical way. 'Barnabas took him and brought him to the apostles' (Acts 9:27)—and he persuaded them to accept him. He told them the story of what Christ had done for Saul—'how he had seen the Lord on the road, and that he had spoken to him'—and what Saul had done for Christ—'how he had preached boldly at Damascus in the name of Jesus'.

Paul completes the story in Galatians. He tells us there that three years passed between his conversion and his first visit to Jerusalem, and that on this visit to Jerusalem, he saw only Peter and James (Galatians 1:15–19). But those two 'pillars of the church' were sufficient. Saul was admitted into the fellowship in Jerusalem: 'He was with them at Jerusalem, coming in and going out. And he spoke boldly in the name of the Lord Jesus …' (Acts 9:28–29).

Now what are we to learn from this?

THE WELCOMING CHURCH

Firstly, we should welcome new converts into our churches.

There are two sides to this. On the one hand we do have to be careful. Most churches interview those who wish to join them, to ensure that they are truly converted—and rightly so. One venerable commentator (Gill) commends the Jerusalem church for their caution, and deduces that 'such persons who, before a profession of religion, have been either very scandalous ... or notorious enemies to Christ ... ought to be thoroughly examined into'.[1]

There *is* a need to be careful, and we ought not to be too quick to condemn the Jerusalem church for being wary of Saul. Paul himself warned the Ephesian elders about 'savage wolves' (Acts 20:29). Church leaders have a responsibility to protect the flock.

We need also to protect people from self-deception. There are some who think they are Christians, when they are not. For their own sake, we need to show them their need to be converted.

On the other hand, Saul *was* genuinely converted. The need here was for generosity of spirit, and openness of heart—for a willingness to believe the unbelievable, and to accept that even *this* man could be saved.

Barnabas was able to make that leap of imagination.

This was one of the qualities he would later need as a missionary. It took a remarkable leap of faith to believe that the Gentiles of Cyprus and of Asia Minor could actually become Christians. There were many, especially in Jerusalem, who could not come to terms with this. But the man who could believe that a Pharisee might be converted could also hope for the conversion of the Gentiles! How we need that spirit today.

Now if Saul was converted, he should be welcomed. It was as simple as that. It was said of our Lord, in Luke 15:2, 'This man receives sinners'. We must do the same. As Paul says in Romans 15:7, 'Receive one another, just as Christ also received us, to the glory of God.'

SPIRITUAL DISCERNMENT

Secondly, we need discernment to know when someone is saved.

Barnabas had this discernment. He was convinced that Saul was converted, despite the scepticism of others. This was not just wishful thinking—wanting to believe it, regardless of the evidence. He had considered the evidence and recognized God's work in this man. He had seen what others were unable to see—and, of course, subsequent history proved him right.

This too was a quality he would need later as a missionary; it is a quality we will see at work again in the next chapter. It is a quality we need today.

There is much in the church to be cautious about—but often we are suspicious and sceptical when we ought to be rejoicing; negative and critical when we ought to be praising God; doubtful and cautious when we ought to be amazed at what God has done; despondent and depressed when we ought to be expecting great things from God.

But we need discernment to know what is genuine and what is not.

TRUE FRIENDSHIP

Thirdly, we have here a wonderful lesson in friendship. Here was Saul, lonely and rejected—how he needed a friend! Barnabas stood by him as a true friend—one who accepted him, believed him, and was willing to take risks for him.

And it was a risk. The apostles could easily have rejected not only Saul, but Barnabas as well. They could have laughed at his gullibility;

they could have dismissed him as lacking in discernment; they could even have suspected him of being an infiltrator himself, led astray by Saul. He was putting his own reputation on the line—but that is what friends do.

Again, he is showing the character of Christ, the friend of sinners. Our Lord Jesus Christ is the 'friend indeed' who will stand by us in our hour of need. That is what Barnabas did for Saul.

THE POWER OF PERSUASION

Finally, we see here the power of persuasion. Barnabas argued Saul's case, and persuaded the apostles to accept him. Given the case against Saul, that was no easy task. But that is the task of an advocate: to plead a client's case, however difficult it may be.

Once again, it is the character of Christ shining through. Christ is our advocate above, pleading for us with the Father; here is Barnabas, a true disciple of Christ, doing the same for Saul. Would you do the same?

Notes

1 *Gill's Exposition of the Old and New Testaments* on Acts 9, Vol. 8 (Primitive Baptist Library, 1976), p. 229.

Apostolic ambassador

Acts 11:21–30

There is a principle in Christian work (indeed, in life in general) that 'He who is faithful in what is least is faithful also in much; and he who is unjust in what is least is unjust also in much' (Luke 16:10).

Barnabas had been faithful in using his wealth; he had also been faithful in standing up for Saul. Now he is given a greater task.

A new church in Antioch

The dispersion of the church because of Saul's persecution had unexpected consequences. The gospel had actually spread!

Now those who were scattered after the persecution that arose over Stephen travelled as far as Phoenicia, Cyprus, and Antioch, preaching the word to no one but the Jews only. But some of them were men from Cyprus and Cyrene, who, when they had come to Antioch, spoke to the Hellenists, preaching the Lord Jesus. And the hand of the Lord was with them, and a great number believed and turned to the Lord (Acts 11:19–21).

Here is a remarkable instance of God's sovereignty. Persecution in Jerusalem, which was intended to wipe out the church, had instead forced the church to expand into new territory. Saul's attempt to stop this 'error' had prompted them to fulfil the Great Commission in ways they might otherwise not have thought of. 'He who sits in the heavens shall laugh; the LORD shall hold them in derision'

(Psalm 2:4). God always has 'the last laugh' on those who oppose him!

These unknown missionaries took the initiative themselves—there is no suggestion of an apostolic plan. But no doubt they remembered our Lord's plan—'You shall be witnesses to me in Jerusalem, and in all Judea and Samaria, and to the end of the earth' (Acts 1:8).

Luke says that they 'preached' the Lord Jesus. The Greek word used here, however, is the ordinary word for talking. It has been described as 'gossiping the gospel'.

They also took a significant new step—they spoke to the 'Hellenists'. This could mean simply Greek-speaking Jews, but the AV translates it 'Grecians', and some ancient manuscripts do actually have the word 'Greeks'. The contrast between 'Jews only' (v. 19) and 'Hellenists' favours this more radical interpretation—these men preached to the Gentiles.

Now this was not the first time the gospel had been preached to the Gentiles. Acts 10–11 tells the story of Peter preaching to Cornelius. That was the real breakthrough, the 'Gentile Pentecost', when the Spirit fell upon the Gentiles just as he had upon the Jewish disciples at the beginning.

But now, for the first time, large numbers of Gentiles came to the Lord. Indeed, the church at Antioch must have been predominantly Gentile.

Coming to terms with a new work

When 'news of these things came to the ears of the church in Jerusalem' (11:22), it must have caused a stir.

The church at Jerusalem had given Peter quite a grilling for going to Cornelius. Separation from the Gentiles was a major principle in

Judaism, and the church had been slow to broaden its vision—despite numerous hints in the Old Testament that God would save the Gentiles (Genesis 12:3; Psalm 2:8; Isaiah 45:22; Jonah 4:11, etc.) and our Lord's own claim to be the Saviour of the world (John 3:16). After Peter's account of the conversion of Cornelius, they had glorified God, saying, 'Then God has also granted to the Gentiles repentance to life' (Acts 11:18). But was this a one-off, an exception, or were the Gentiles about to come flooding into the church? Events at Antioch seemed to suggest that they were.

No doubt there were many emotions when they heard about Antioch. Some, perhaps, rejoiced; others, perhaps, were sceptical; some may have been apprehensive. It needed investigation.

And so they sent Barnabas.

Barnabas investigates

We are not told what Barnabas' 'terms of reference' were—whether he was merely to inspect the work and report back, or whether he was sent to supervise the work and bring it under apostolic control. It was not, however, a mere private visit. Barnabas was going as an apostolic ambassador.

It is not hard to see why they chose Barnabas.

Firstly, he was from Cyprus. The men who had started this work were 'from Cyprus and Cyrene'. Some of them therefore were his fellow-countrymen. He would get on well with them.

Secondly, Barnabas had a reputation for discernment. He had been right about Saul; he could be relied upon to judge whether this was of God or not.

Discernment is a rare gift. Most ministers have made mistakes, thinking someone was converted when he or she was not (and vice versa); many have made fools of themselves by backing some movement in the church which has subsequently proved a disaster.

We could liken it to an art expert, judging whether a painting really is by Rembrandt, or by one of his pupils, or, worse still, a fraud. You might say that a master's work is self evidently better than any pale imitation—and to the trained eye, it is. I remember watching an amateur artist copying a painting in the National Gallery in London, and feeling slightly embarrassed for him. It was better than anything I could have done, but hopelessly inferior to the original. But faced only with the copy, I might have been fooled. Likewise in spiritual things—it requires a trained eye to discern what is genuine. Barnabas was the expert!

Thirdly, Barnabas was the 'Son of Encouragement'. If the work was genuine, Barnabas was the man to encourage these new converts.

Sending gentle Barnabas rather than some stern inquisitor was maybe an indication that Jerusalem was inclined to view the new work favourably.

What, then, did Barnabas do? 'When he came and had seen the grace of God, he was glad, and encouraged them all that with purpose of heart they should continue with the Lord' (11:23). In this, he was following the Master: 'Then Jesus said to those Jews who believed him, "If you abide in my word, you are my disciples indeed"' (John 8:31). It is the same advice Paul and Barnabas later gave to the new converts on the first missionary journey: 'They returned to Lystra, Iconium and [Pisidian] Antioch, strengthening the souls of the disciples, exhorting them to continue in the faith' (Acts 14:21–22).

Luke comments that Barnabas 'was a good man, full of the Holy Spirit and of faith' (Acts 11:24)—another wonderful testimonial.

He also adds that 'a great many people were added to the Lord'—perhaps partly through the preaching of Barnabas.

Barnabas the head-hunter

Barnabas recognized, however, that something more was required in Antioch. All these converts needed teaching. And it was too much for Barnabas. He was not too proud to admit that he needed help; he had no desire to 'go it alone'. He needed someone to help teach these people.

Therefore Barnabas turns 'apostolic head-hunter', searching out the right man for the job. And the right man, for Barnabas, is Saul of Tarsus. In 11:25–26, 'Barnabas departed for Tarsus to seek Saul. And when he had found him, he brought him to Antioch. So it was that for a whole year they assembled with the church and taught a great many people.'

It is easy for us to see, in retrospect, why Saul was the man for Antioch. Here was a church, predominantly Gentile, and there was a man called to the Gentiles—it was a perfect match. But we have the benefit of knowing only the main characters—we can only think of one candidate! Imagine Barnabas, with all his contacts in Jerusalem and, perhaps, across the water in Cyprus. It was not so easy for him to choose. But choose he did, and again he showed great discernment.

That year in Antioch must have been wonderful—imagine Barnabas and Paul as your regular preachers! The church grew, and made an impression—'The disciples were first called Christians in Antioch' (11:26). Probably this name was meant as an insult, but they were happy to accept it. That is what they were—followers of Christ, trusting in Christ for their salvation, and seeking to imitate Christ. And few deserved the name more than Barnabas—a true Christian, teaching others to be Christians.

Barnabas the courier

A year on, however, another challenge arose. Time never stands still, and a year is a long time in the New Testament!

I remember, as a new pastor, being asked to give my 'initial impressions' after two years in the ministry. I am not defending short pastorates, but only once did Paul ever stay longer than two years in one place!

We must be ready always to meet the needs of the hour, and a fresh need had arisen for Barnabas to respond to.

Various prophets had come from Jerusalem, and one of them, Agabus, had predicted a great famine throughout the Roman world (11:28).

This famine actually happened in the days of Claudius, in AD 46. It is mentioned by the Jewish historian Josephus, who tells us that Queen Helena of Adiabene, having adopted Judaism, helped the Jews in Jerusalem by buying grain from Alexandria and figs from Cyprus (*Antiquities*, Part 20). The Roman historians Suteonius (*Life of Claudius* chapter 18) and Tacitus (*Annals* 11:4) also mention it.

The church at Antioch, being open to the voice of the Spirit, believed this prophecy and determined to respond. Antioch was wealthy; but there was deep concern for the church in Judea. Therefore, 'each according to his ability', they 'determined to send relief to the brethren dwelling in Judea', and they 'sent it to the elders by the hands of Barnabas and Saul' (11:29–30).

This lovely generosity reflects the generosity of Barnabas himself—no doubt he had taught them to share with the poor.

But for Barnabas, it meant another journey to Jerusalem—such was the importance of this gift that they sent their most prominent men. No doubt also it was a large sum of money, and they wanted someone reliable. Barnabas had proved himself trustworthy in financial matters; he had proved also, by selling his own land, that he was not covetous. They could trust Barnabas!

When he returned, a whole new phase would begin in his life.

Once again, there is much to learn, None of us, of course, will ever be called to be an apostolic ambassador. But there are some abiding principles here.

FAITHFULNESS

Firstly, there is the importance of faithfulness. Whatever the Lord gives us to do, we must do it with all our might, taking each task as it comes. Barnabas was diligent in everything he did—whether it was teaching the church, or delivering a gift, it was the Lord's work.

As Christians, we must fulfil the ministry the Lord has given us, however great or small. And if we are faithful in the small tasks, it may well be that the Lord will give us greater tasks.

ENTHUSIASM

Secondly, we should be enthusiastic about all that the Lord is doing, whether or not we are involved ourselves.

Barnabas was enthusiastic about the work in Antioch from day one, even though it was not his work. He 'was glad' when he saw the grace of God. Sadly, there is among some Christians a narrow perspective, which rejoices only in their own work, and pours scorn upon anything else.

There was no 'ministerial jealousy' with Barnabas, resenting the fact that these converts had been made by someone else. He was simply delighted that the Lord was at work, and happy to help in any way he could. What an example to us all!

RIGHT MAN, RIGHT PLACE, RIGHT TIME

Thirdly, there is the importance of being in the right ministry.

Barnabas was 'the right man for the job' of going to Antioch initially; Saul was 'the right man for the job' of teaching at Antioch.

Suppose Barnabas had been left in Jerusalem to supervise the distribution of food—which would have been a very logical choice of ministry for him. We can imagine that he would have done the job cheerfully; no doubt he would have done it well—but it was not what he was called to do. Someone among the apostles (maybe all of them!) had the imagination to see Barnabas as the man for Antioch, and sent him there.

Similarly, suppose Saul had been left in Tarsus to ponder on his future mission to the Gentiles. Would it ever have happened? Saul needed to go to Antioch, and Antioch needed Saul.

The most obvious application today is in choosing a pastor. Any church which has faced this challenge, under any system of church government, will know how difficult it is, and how often we get it wrong; and both the church and the misplaced pastor suffer.

Equally in other ministries, we need to put people in the right jobs. This is the duty of the elders, but also as individuals we have a responsibility to seek the mind of the Lord. How we need discernment, to place people where they ought to be!

Remember too that time marches on. Needs change. We must be in the right place at the right time, and always ready for a new challenge.

THE CRY FOR TEACHERS

Fourthly, there is a need for teachers. These new converts in Antioch could not teach themselves. They needed Barnabas and Saul.

This is the cry of many churches today. There are many parts of the world—often the poorer countries—where the Lord has poured out blessing in revival. There are many converts, but few teachers. They are often like sheep without a shepherd, wandering unsuspectingly into whatever false doctrine comes their way. They need teachers.

And so do we. Pray for more men like Barnabas and Saul.

REMEMBER THE POOR

Fifthly, 'remember the poor' (Galatians 2:10). Barnabas and Saul were just as concerned for the poor in Judea as for the work in Antioch.

Today, there are famines in many parts of the world, on a scale that would have staggered Agabus. Quite apart from our general duty to the poor, there are many Christians in those countries. Should we not be helping our 'poor brethren'? People sometimes say, 'Evangelism is more important.' But surely, it is not 'either/or'—both are important.

A TRUE CHRISTIAN

Finally, live up to your name! The disciples were 'first called Christians' in Antioch, and Barnabas, no doubt, lived up to that name.

If you have trusted in Christ as your Lord and Saviour, you *are* a Christian. But do you live up to the name? Many Christians, sadly, bring shame on the name of Christ by their behaviour. Others are so quiet about their faith, you would never know they were Christians.

Everyone would have known that Barnabas was a Christian! Not only did he talk about Christ, he was also a follower of Christ in all that he did.

The name 'Christian' is precious. Treasure it, and live up to it!

Missionary call

Acts 13:2

We come now to a whole new chapter in the story of Barnabas—his call to the mission field.

Everything so far could be seen as a preparation for this. The sale of his lands in Acts 4 would have prepared him for life in the mission field without a settled home; his friendship with Saul prepared him to work alongside this 'chosen vessel' of God. Speaking up for Saul in Jerusalem would have prepared him for often delicate relationships with the churches; his ministry in Antioch would have prepared him for teaching Gentile converts.

Saul had also been prepared—learning from the start how to preach and how to suffer for the name of Christ.

The Lord had chosen them both beforehand for missionary work; for years he had been preparing them, giving them both progressively greater responsibilities; now they were ready—it was time to go.

It is doubtful whether Barnabas would have seen this as 'becoming a missionary'. So far as he was concerned, it was probably just a new work.

The word 'missionary', surprisingly, is not found in the New Testament. It is actually a relatively modern word. The word 'mission' was first used (of the Jesuits) in 1598, and the word 'missionary' in 1656. It comes from the Latin *missio* and means literally 'one who is sent'. The equivalent word in the New Testament is 'apostle', from the Greek *apostolos*, which also means 'one who is sent'. Barnabas is actually called an apostle in Acts 14:4 and 14, though we hesitate, perhaps, to use the word, because of its more restricted reference to the Twelve (and Paul).

Whichever word we use, however, Barnabas and Saul were sent, both by the Lord and by the church, to preach the gospel to the Gentiles.

To understand what happened, we must backtrack briefly to Acts 12.

The background

Acts 12 describes events in Jerusalem around AD 44—the martyrdom of James and the extraordinary escape of Peter from prison, followed by the death of Herod.

Now Barnabas and Saul had been sent to Jerusalem with relief for the poor in chapter 11. Probably the obvious place for them to stay would have been the house of John Mark, Barnabas' cousin—which was the very location of the famous prayer meeting in 12:12, where Peter suddenly appeared just as they were praying for him.

We cannot say whether Barnabas and Saul were actually present at that meeting, but it must have been the 'talk of the town', and they must have heard of it. Luke's vivid account may owe something to Paul's memory, whether he knew of it first or second hand.

What we do know is that when they returned, mission accomplished, to Antioch, they took John Mark with them—'Barnabas and Saul returned from Jerusalem when they had fulfilled their ministry, and they also took with them John whose surname was Mark' (12:25).

The word 'ministry' here, incidentally, is *diakonia* in Greek; this effectively was their 'diaconate'. They were not too proud to act as 'deacons'!

Now John Mark was about to become their assistant. We cannot help wondering whether they had discussed with him what they hoped to do—the Bible does not say.

The call

The call came shortly after their return—and it came at a ministers' meeting. 'In the church that was at Antioch there were certain prophets and teachers: Barnabas, Simeon who was called Niger, Lucius of Cyrene, Manaen who had been brought up with Herod the tetrarch, and Saul. As they ministered to the Lord and fasted', the Holy Spirit spoke (13:1–2).

This impressive array of names reminds us that the New Testament knows nothing of a one-man ministry!

Barnabas is listed first, presumably as the most senior among them.

Simeon Niger ('black') may perhaps have been African, perhaps from Cyrene (now Libya), as Cyrenians were among the founders of the church. (Some have speculated that he may have been Simon the Cyrenian who carried the cross, but that seems unlikely.)

Lucius *was* a Cyrenian, perhaps a 'founder member' of the church.

Manaen was literally the 'foster brother' of Herod—not the Herod who had just died (ch. 12), but Herod Antipas, who ruled in our Lord's lifetime. Christianity evidently had reached the royal household! Saul is listed last, perhaps as the youngest.

Who were the prophets and who the teachers, we are not told; perhaps they were all prophets *and* teachers.

That day, it seems, they had met to worship; the impression is given that they often met in this way. While they were worshipping, the Holy Spirit spoke—probably through one of the prophets: 'Now separate to me Barnabas and Saul for the work to which I have called them' (13:2).

Notice that God had *already* called them. When? In Saul's case, we know, because he has told us. God had chosen Saul for this work before he was converted, and he revealed it to him right at the start. In Acts 9:15, we read that the Lord said to Ananias, 'Go, for he is a chosen vessel of mine to bear my name before Gentiles, kings, and the children of Israel.' And Ananias had told Saul, 'The God of our fathers has chosen you that you should know his will, and see the Just One, and hear the voice of his mouth. For you will be his witness to all men of what you have seen and heard' (22:14–15). Later, the Lord confirmed it to him in a vision in the temple: 'Depart, for I will send you far from here to the Gentiles' (22:17–21).

But what about Barnabas? The Lord must have spoken to Barnabas in some way, to justify the words, 'the work to which I have called *them*'. But we are not told how or when this happened. These personal details are not revealed to us. Luke probably did not know. Luke joined Paul only in Acts 16, after Paul and Barnabas had separated, and may have either not known Barnabas personally, or not had opportunity to ask him.

But Barnabas undoubtedly knew in his own heart that he was called to this work—as, indeed, every missionary surely does today.

A variety of experiences

With a missionary call (or any other call into Christian work), as with conversion, it is the genuineness of the call that matters, rather than the circumstances—*what* has happened, rather than *how* it happened. Missionary testimonies are very varied.

William Carey first heard the call to mission quietly in his own heart while working as a cobbler and schoolmaster in Moulton, and as the pastor of a small Baptist congregation. The call came through reading *The Last Voyage of Captain Cook*, which awakened him to the needs of a world without Christ. He concluded, 'If it be the duty of all men to believe the gospel … then it be the duty of those who are entrusted with the gospel to endeavour to make it known among all nations', and he prayed, 'Here am I; send me!' At first he met with little encouragement. When he spoke on the subject at a meeting of ministers, he was allegedly rebuked by an older minister: 'Young man, sit down: when God pleases to convert the heathen, he will do it without your aid or mine'—so different from the meeting in Antioch! But he persevered, publishing his famous *Enquiry* in 1791, urging the church to action, and eventually he prevailed—the Particular Baptist Society for the Propagation of the Gospel Among the Heathen was formed in 1792, and Carey went to India in 1793.

David Livingstone likewise was moved by the needs of mission, though, in his case, it was the appeals of missionaries themselves that moved him. Having read Karl Gutzlaff's *Appeal in behalf of China*, Livingstone resolved to go there, giving as his reason 'the claims of so many millions of his fellow-creatures, and the complaint of the want of qualified men to undertake the task'. The Opium Wars, however, made it impossible, and he turned his attention to Africa. He had met Robert Moffat, who told him that he had 'sometimes seen in the morning sun the smoke of a thousand villages where no missionary had ever been'. The rest is history!

Hudson Taylor could trace his call back to childhood. His father was deeply concerned for the spiritual needs of China, and, at the age of five, he had said he would like one day to be a missionary to China! But the call only became clear in 1849, when he was seventeen. After reading a tract on the finished work of Christ, he finally understood what Christ had done for him, and at once gave himself to the service of Christ.

There are patterns here, but each case is different. God deals with his servants as individuals. The call often comes, however, long before the work begins—sometimes many years beforehand.

The church dimension

What happens in Acts 13 is not strictly the call, but the commissioning: '*Set apart* for me Barnabas and Saul.' It is the church dimension in the missionary call.

Barnabas and Saul could simply have announced that the Lord had called them, and then gone off into the work, but no—they must wait until the church (represented by the prophets and teachers) recognizes their call. Even in mission, we must act not just as individuals, but as members of the church.

The church, however, must also respond promptly when the Lord speaks—and these leaders in Antioch did. In 13:3, 'having fasted and prayed, and laid hands on them, they sent them away.' Paul could say later, 'I was not disobedient to the heavenly vision' (26:19); neither was the church.

The laying-on of hands, of course, was the customary way of identifying with a person; symbolically, blessing flowed through those hands. Undoubtedly they had prayed for God's blessing upon this mission.

There are many lessons in all this; let me choose three.

ARE WE LISTENING?

Barnabas and Saul began their missionary work in answer to a call. In

Saul's case, that involved listening, first to Ananias, then to the Lord in a vision, and then to the Spirit in the meeting in Antioch—in each case recognizing the voice of his Master.

Are we listening to the Lord today?

Are we listening to the Holy Spirit, as we read the Bible—as he lays on our hearts, perhaps, the importance of mission? Are we listening to our friends, when they talk to us about mission, and suggest, perhaps, that we might be called to it? Are we listening to the appeals of missionaries, when they come home on furlough and plead with us to pray for 'the Lord of the harvest to send out labourers' into their harvest fields (Matthew 9:38)? Are we listening to the church, when the elders suggest we might be called? Are we praying (and fasting?) to know the Lord's will?

Many of us, perhaps, have made our minds up about what we are going to do in life. We are settled into a comfortable career, with no thought or desire for missionary work, and we are just not listening.

Praise God that Barnabas and Saul listened!

ARE WE WILLING?

When we read through Acts, it all seems so simple. The Lord speaks and the disciples go—as simple as that!

In reality, it was not that easy.

Imagine how hard it must have been for Barnabas and Saul to leave such a successful ministry in Antioch for the uncertainty of the Gentile world. Here they had a regular, appreciative congregation; there, for all they knew, they might be rejected and stoned by an angry mob. Here, they were just a few days' journey from Jerusalem; there, they might be out of touch with everyone they knew for months on end. Yet they went, because the Lord had called them.

Imagine how hard it must have been for the church in Antioch to part with two of their best teachers. How would they manage without them? The church by now may have numbered thousands, yet there were only five names on that list in Acts 13—and now two of them were going. But they allowed them to go—indeed, they sent them away with their blessing—because the Lord had called them.

Are we willing to obey the voice of the Lord?

What he says we will do,
Where he sends we will go—
Never fear, only trust and obey.[1]

WHO SENDS OUT THE MISSIONARIES?

There has been a great emphasis in recent years on church-based mission. The local church, we are told, must send out the missionaries, and, as far as possible, support and direct them; Acts 13 is often quoted as a basis for this argument. By and large, this is a helpful emphasis. It is not good that missionaries should go out as 'Lone Rangers', and it is hard to find biblical support for missionary societies acting independently of the local church. But we must maintain the biblical balance.

Barnabas and Saul were *first* called by the Lord, and *then* sent by the church. Indeed, strictly speaking, they were sent by the Lord, since the church itself merely acted in obedience to the Lord.

It is very striking to compare verse 3 with verse 4. In verse 3, the prophets and teachers '… laid hands on them [and] sent them away'. But immediately afterwards, in verse 4, they are described as 'sent out *by the Holy Spirit*'.

Who, then, sent them? Both the church *and* the Spirit—not acting separately or independently from each other, but together, in perfect harmony: the church obeying the Spirit.

There is an interesting parallel with Revelation 22:17. There, 'The Spirit and the bride say, "Come!"' Here, the Spirit and the bride say, 'Go!'

Without the Spirit, the mission would have been a complete failure—as Jesus said, 'Without me you can do nothing' (John 15:5). But, equally, without the church, they would have had a very difficult time. The church is the body of Christ, and one member cannot easily act without the others.

Barnabas and Saul were the Lord's missionaries, not the church's missionaries. This is emphasized by the wording of the call in verse 2: 'Separate *to me* Barnabas and Saul ...' Not, 'separate to yourselves', or even, 'separate to the work', but 'separate to me ... for the work'.

The church at Antioch had the privilege and joy of sending them out, and one would assume that they supported them—though this is never explicitly stated. There is, however, no suggestion that the church ever attempted to direct the work. Barnabas and Saul went where the Lord directed them. At the end of their mission, they reported back to Antioch (14:26–27). Otherwise the church remains in the background.

We cannot construct hard and fast rules from one example, but this does seem to be the biblical pattern: the local church confirms and supports the individual call to mission.

Of course there are exceptions. Many faithful missionaries have gone out without support, because the local church failed to 'catch the vision'.

Of course there is a role for missionary societies. Who would deny the tremendous influence for good of the London Missionary Society, the China Inland Mission, and other great missionary organizations? A large church like that in Antioch could give Saul and Barnabas all the support they needed, but many small churches cannot do this. Missionary societies enable them to do so.

But, undoubtedly, the biblical pattern here in Acts 13 is for the local church to support and encourage the God-called missionary.

May there be many like Barnabas and Saul sent out in our days!

Notes

1 **John Henry Sammis,** *When we walk with the Lord.*

Paul's companion in Cyprus

Acts 13:4–12

From Acts 13 onwards, the apostle Paul takes centre stage. (He is called 'Saul' up to 13:7, and then 'Paul' after that.) We ought never to forget that he had other companions with him. He needed them, and they shared in the work. However, on the first missionary journey, in Acts 13 and 14, his constant companion was Barnabas.

Indeed, Barnabas is named before Saul on the first stage of the mission, in Cyprus, in 13:7—as he has been all along so far (11:30; 12:25; 13:2). We ought really to think of Saul as Barnabas' companion in Cyprus!

It all changes in verse 13, when they sail away from Cyprus to Perga in Pamphylia. Saul is now called Paul, and the Bible speaks of 'Paul and his party'.

It would be inappropriate here to look at every detail in the first missionary journey—that belongs to a book on Paul. However, we will look briefly at what happened, from Barnabas' point of view— after all, he was there all the way through.

A missionary to his own homeland

In 13:4–5, 'Being sent out by the Holy Spirit, they went down to Seleucia, and from there they sailed to Cyprus. And when they arrived in Salamis, they preached the word of God in the synagogues of the Jews. They also had John as their assistant.' They travelled through the whole island, until they came to Paphos, and there they encountered Elymas the sorcerer.

We cannot emphasize enough the importance of those opening

words, 'sent ... by the Holy Spirit'. Without that, the entire mission would have failed. We need to understand, in all our ceaseless activity in this hectic age, that the Holy Spirit is essential.

Much of our disappointment probably results from our failure to remember this. We plan and we work without seeking the mind of the Lord. We do what seems good in our own eyes, and then hope that the Lord will bless. But he will only bless what he has commanded.

Barnabas and Saul went out at the Lord's command, and with the Lord's blessing—and their mission was a success.

Now Cyprus, of course, was Barnabas' home country. It was also the first port of call in any journey from Antioch to the west.

They could, if they had wished, have travelled overland, through Cilicia, which was Paul's home country; but they chose this more direct route.

For Barnabas, this was a gentle introduction to missionary work. This was 'home from home'. He was born in Cyprus and may still have had relatives there; he knew this area; he knew these people. It may well be that he was known in these synagogues, and welcomed as a 'local boy'.

It was also a gentle introduction for 'John'—that is, John Mark, who went with them as their 'assistant'. John Mark was related to Barnabas—Colossians 4:10 calls him his 'cousin' (NKJV, NIV), or 'sister's son' (AV).

There is, however, no mention of a family visit. They may or may not have visited relatives; we do not know. Luke is only concerned with the work.

Through the island

They began in Salamis, a seaport at the eastern end of the island. There, they 'preached the word of God in the synagogues', following, no doubt, Paul's principle of 'the Jew first' (Romans 1:16). Nothing is said of the Gentiles.

They were not the first to come to Cyprus. In 11:19 we are told, 'Those who were scattered after the persecution that arose over Stephen travelled as far as ... Cyprus ... preaching the word to no one but the Jews only'. Ironically, these missionaries were forced out by Paul before his conversion; now Paul himself had come there. There were surely converts from this earlier work; no mention is made, however, of any churches.

From Salamis they travelled through the island—no doubt preaching as they went—to Paphos, another seaport, at the western end. Paul, as always, was very thorough!

Conflict and success

Here in Paphos, the first significant incident took place. 'They found a certain sorcerer, a false prophet, a Jew whose name was Bar-Jesus, who was with the proconsul, Sergius Paulus, an intelligent man. This man called for Barnabas and Saul and sought to hear the word of God. But Elymas the sorcerer (for so his name is translated) withstood them, seeking to turn the proconsul away from the faith' (13:6–8).

It may, perhaps, come as a surprise to find a Jewish sorcerer, given the stern prohibition of sorcery in the Law of Moses. Deuteronomy 18:10–12 is quite clear: 'There shall not be found among you anyone who ... practises witchcraft, or a soothsayer, or one who interprets omens, or a sorcerer ... All who do these things are an abomination to the Lord'. These occult practices were common in pagan society, but forbidden in Israel. How could Elymas, as a Jew, justify being a sorcerer?

Sinful man can always find an excuse for his behaviour, and no doubt Elymas had convinced himself that what he was doing was lawful. Likewise today, it is astonishing how 'Christians' can convince themselves that almost any kind of ungodliness is acceptable.

This man was a hindrance to the gospel, actively discouraging Sergius Paulus from following Christ. He was an antichrist in every sense: a false prophet, whereas Christ is the true Prophet; a magician, whereas Christ worked real miracles; a false substitute and an enemy of Christ. Even his name, Elymas Bar-Jesus ('son of Jesus') might have sown confusion in the proconsul's mind.

It was necessary for Paul vigorously to oppose this man—and that is what he did, in the power of the Spirit. 'Then Saul, who also is called Paul, filled with the Holy Spirit, looked intently at him and said, "O full of all deceit and all fraud, you son of the devil, you enemy of all righteousness, will you not cease perverting the straight ways of the Lord? And now, indeed, the hand of the Lord is upon you, and you shall be blind, not seeing the sun for a time"'. Elymas was struck blind, and the proconsul believed (13:9–12).

Now Barnabas was present throughout all this, looking on, no doubt as amazed as everyone else. It is hard to imagine gentle Barnabas speaking this way—but someone had to. Barnabas, quite rightly, allows Paul to handle this one—that is his gift.

One can only imagine the delight Barnabas must have felt at the conversion of the proconsul. Coming from Cyprus, he must surely have been concerned for those who ruled the island. He may not have known Sergius Paulus personally (proconsuls came and went, and Barnabas had been away for some while), but he would surely have prayed for those in authority. 'I exhort first of all that supplications, prayers, intercessions, and giving of thanks be made for all men—for kings and all who are in authority,' Paul later wrote (1 Timothy 2:1–2). Why not pray for their conversion?

This was the first 'high-profile' convert to Christianity—the first of many. 'All kings shall fall down before him; all nations shall serve him' (Psalm 72:11). The Lord had said concerning Paul, 'He is a chosen vessel of mine to bear my name before Gentiles, kings, and the children of Israel' (Acts 9:15). Here was the first Gentile ruler to be converted.

In 1877, an inscription was found to Sergius Paulus in Paphos; a memorial stone in Rome records that in AD 47 he became keeper of one of the riverbanks of the Tiber; another stone inscription from Pisidian Antioch (now in the Yalvac museum in Turkey) also mentions him. His family had large landholdings in Pisidian Antioch—which (significantly?) was where Paul and Barnabas went next.

From this time on Saul is always called Paul. Some think he may have adopted his name from Sergius Paulus; others think he had always had the two names, one Hebrew, one Roman (being a Roman citizen, as well as a Jew), and that it was simply more expedient to use the Roman name now that he was among Gentiles. The name 'Paul' means 'little', and tradition has it that he was a little man; he saw himself also as 'less than the least of all the saints' (Ephesians 3:8)—though we might think differently! Also, from this time onward, Paul takes the lead and Barnabas becomes simply 'Paul's companion'.

It is time to pause and take stock. What have we learned?

OPPORTUNITIES AND OPPOSITION

Paul and Barnabas had no pre-booked meetings in Cyprus, no friendly churches waiting to welcome them, no guarantee that anyone would listen. But opportunities came.

Firstly, there were the obvious opportunities in the synagogues. Every Sabbath, they must have gone to the synagogue praying that they would be invited to speak—it was customary for a visiting rabbi to address the congregation, but only if they were invited. God was with them, giving them favour with the Jewish authorities, opening doors for them to preach the gospel 'to the Jew first'.

Then came that unexpected opportunity to preach to the proconsul. The proconsul, remember, '*called* for Barnabas and Saul', because he *wanted* to hear the word of God. What a surprise that must have been!

When the Holy Spirit is with us, opportunities come.

That is not to say, of course, that we should not *look* for opportunities. When Barnabas and Saul attended the synagogue, they were looking for an opportunity, and if the opportunities had not come, no doubt they would have created some.

But every Christian who sincerely wants to serve God will find that opportunities come. A friend, perhaps, may ask you about your faith; the local church may invite you to preach; or a local radio station may ask you for an interview. Grasp those opportunities with open arms! Within the last year, our own church has been invited to start a Bible club in a local school. The initiative came from the school; there were children there who actually *wanted* a Bible club.

We might think that, in today's world, no one wants to hear the gospel. People are busy; they have other priorities. In any case, fallen men and women are 'dead in trespasses and sins' (Ephesians 2:1), and their hearts are closed to the gospel. But God is constantly at work, opening hearts, and we may be surprised how often the most unlikely people *do* want to hear.

The Roman world was actually no easier than our world today. Sergius Paulus was a busy man, brought up, no doubt, with a pagan worldview, and yet he was open to the gospel. So are many people today.

When the opportunities come, however, we must be ready for them. Just imagine if Paul and Barnabas had arrived at the proconsul's palace, embarrassed and confused, not knowing what to say to such a high official. But they knew what to say. There is one gospel for all mankind; they simply preached this gospel.

'Make the most of every opportunity' (Colossians 4:5, NIV). By seizing the opportunity with Sergius Paulus, Paul and Barnabas show us how to do this.

With the opportunities, however, there will always come opposition. When 'a great door' is opened, there will be 'many adversaries' (1 Corinthians 16:9).

No violent opposition is recorded in the synagogues of Cyprus, but there was Elymas the sorcerer. Paul and Barnabas were faced with the occult; they were opposed by the devil. But Christ said, 'I will build my church, and the gates of Hades shall not prevail against it' (Matthew 16:18).

They were also facing a Jew who had brought discredit upon religion, who had obscured the truth by his own ungodly behaviour. This, perhaps, is one of the greatest hindrances we have to contend with today—ungodly Christians who have put people off Christianity. But the Spirit of God can overcome this.

How careful we must be that we are not a hindrance to the gospel ourselves!

HUMILITY AND HONOUR

Here in Acts 13, Barnabas has to take second place to the apostle Paul. What humility that must have required!

Barnabas was presumably the older man, and the more experienced Christian; without him Paul might never have been in the church at all. It was Barnabas who had persuaded the church at Jerusalem to accept Paul; it was Barnabas who had brought Paul to Antioch. His name had appeared at the head of the list of prophets and teachers in Acts 13:1; his name had been mentioned first by the Holy Spirit in the call to missionary work: 'Separate to me Barnabas and Saul for the work to which I have called them' (13:2).

And yet, now it was Paul who was taking the lead, pronouncing judgement upon Elymas.

At least here in Cyprus—his home territory—Barnabas is still mentioned first. But even that is about to change. From the moment they leave Cyprus, 'Barnabas and Saul' become 'Paul and Barnabas'.

One of the hardest tests of holiness is how we react when others overtake us—when other Christians have more success in their ministry, when a younger Christian is preferred for some office in the church, when others are praised, and we feel neglected, or when the gifts of other Christians make them more prominent, while ours go unnoticed.

John the Baptist is the supreme example. In John 3:26, his disciples told him, 'Rabbi, he who was with you beyond the Jordan, to whom you have testified—behold, he is baptizing, and all are coming to him!' They were jealous for John, and apparently could not even bring themselves to say the name of Jesus—he was 'he who was with you'. But John replied, 'A man can receive nothing unless it has been given to him from heaven ... He must increase, but I must decrease' (John 3:27,30).

That is always the spirit we must have—a spirit of humility.

Barnabas seems never to have complained about Paul taking the lead; on the contrary, I am sure he rejoiced that this young man was at last exercising the ministry to which he was called. He seems to have been happy to fade into the background and provide a supporting ministry. God was glorified; people were saved; that was all that mattered.

And God honoured him. His name remains on the pages of Scripture; his role is recognized at every turn. Some historians, perhaps, would have airbrushed Barnabas out of missionary history. Paul is such a towering figure that he alone would be mentioned. But Luke, under the guidance of the Spirit, makes sure that Barnabas is mentioned: 'Honour to whom honour [is due]' (Romans 13:7). Paul takes the lead—but we honour Barnabas, Paul's faithful companion.

Paul's companion on the mainland

Acts 13:13–14:20

S uccess in Paphos was followed by disappointment. How often our lives follow this roller-coaster pattern—riding high and then sinking low! Paul and his companions, Barnabas and John Mark, 'set sail ... to Perga in Pamphylia; and John, departing from them, returned to Jerusalem' (13:13).

Heartbreak

Luke, who had heard the story from Paul, records this news dispassionately—but what a heartbreak this must have been to Barnabas! Remember, John Mark was his cousin (or nephew), and probably his protégé. He loved this young man, not only as family, but as a promising young Christian. Now he had deserted them.

Why John Mark returned to Jerusalem, we are not told. There could be many reasons. Maybe family duties demanded it. Maybe he had not anticipated a longer mission, but had only expected to go to Cyprus. Maybe he was weary of the work. Maybe he was unwell.

Whatever it was, he had decided to go home—and to Paul's mind, that was desertion. Later it led to a major quarrel between Paul and Barnabas—in 15:38, 'Paul insisted that they should not take with them the one who had departed from them in Pamphylia, and had not gone with them to the work.'

Our Lord himself said in Luke 9:62, 'No one, having put his hand to the plough, and looking back, is fit for the kingdom of God'. Paul took the same attitude.

Pisidian Antioch

After John Mark left them, Barnabas remained loyal, and travelled on with Paul to Pisidian Antioch. Here, as their custom was, they went to the synagogue, and were invited to speak: 'Men and brethren, if you have any word of exhortation [or encouragement] for the people, say on' (v. 15). That sounds like a cue for Barnabas, the 'Son of Encouragement', but it is Paul who speaks.

We need not look in detail at his sermon—this is a book about Barnabas! Paul takes them through the Old Testament, showing them how the ancient promises to Israel are fulfilled in Jesus: 'We declare to you glad tidings—that promise which was made to the fathers. God has fulfilled this for us their children, in that he has raised up Jesus' (vv. 32–33).

Notice the plural 'we'. Just as Peter stood up 'with the eleven' on the Day of Pentecost (2:14), so Paul includes Barnabas in his speech. Paul is the speaker, but Barnabas is 100 per cent with him.

Afterwards, Paul and Barnabas left the synagogue together (v. 42) and the people invited them (plural again!) to speak further with them. 'Many of the Jews and devout proselytes [converts to Judaism] followed Paul and Barnabas, who, speaking to them, persuaded them to continue in the grace of God' (v. 43).

Again, both of them shared in this ministry.

The next Sabbath, 'almost the whole city came together to hear the word of God', but the Jews, filled with jealousy, opposed what Paul was saying. Then, 'Paul and Barnabas grew bold and said "It was necessary that the word of God should be spoken to you first; but since you reject it, and judge yourselves unworthy of everlasting life, behold, we turn to the Gentiles"' (v. 46). Again, Paul (we assume) was the speaker, but Barnabas was with him, wholeheartedly endorsing every word. Even gentle Barnabas could pronounce the word of judgement when necessary.

Persecution followed: 'The Jews stirred up the devout and prominent women and the chief men of the city, raised up persecution against Paul and Barnabas, and expelled them from their region' (v. 50).

They left, shaking the dust from their feet, as Jesus had commanded (Luke 9:5), but 'filled with joy and with the Holy Spirit' (v. 52).

Iconium

Next stop was Iconium—modern-day Konya, eighty miles south-east of Antioch. Today it is a Muslim city; the Sufi mystic Rumi is buried there. Then, it was a small provincial town, with a mainly Greek population, and a sizeable Jewish community.

There was a great earthquake in Iconium in 1999; what happened when Paul and Barnabas arrived could be described as a spiritual earthquake. As usual, they went into the synagogue, and there they 'so spoke that a great multitude both of the Jews and of the Greeks believed' (14:1).

Once again, the plural is used—they went in together, and spoke together.

As usual, there was opposition: 'The unbelieving Jews stirred up the Gentiles and poisoned their minds against the brethren' (14:2). Their reaction is remarkable. 'Therefore'—because of the persecution!— 'they stayed there a long time, speaking boldly in the Lord, who was bearing witness to the word of his grace, granting signs and wonders to be done by their hands' (v. 3).

This is the first mention of Barnabas working miracles; indeed, it is also the first mention of Paul working miracles, apart from blinding Elymas.

Paul and Barnabas, quite clearly, were partners in mission. Both preached, and the Lord honoured the preaching of both with conversions, and confirmed the preaching of both with miracles. Hebrews 2:3–4 speaks of 'so great a salvation, which at the first began to be spoken by the Lord, and was confirmed to us by those who heard him, God also bearing witness both with signs and wonders, with various miracles, and gifts of the Holy Spirit, according to his own will.' The Holy Spirit was upon Barnabas just as he was upon on Paul.

They were partners also in suffering. The city was divided, and a plot was hatched 'to abuse and stone them' (Acts 14:5). They were both persecuted.

Now they decided that it was time to go. There was nothing dishonourable in that. Jesus himself said, 'When they persecute you in this city, flee to another' (Matthew 10:23). Mere opposition they could ride out, but death threats were another matter. There was still too much work to be done. And so 'they ... fled to Lystra and Derbe, cities of Lycaonia, and to the surrounding region. And they were preaching the gospel there' (vv. 6–7).

Lystra

Here in Lystra there occurred one of the most remarkable events of the entire journey, one that illustrates vividly the character of Barnabas.

In Lystra they met a man crippled from birth, who sat listening to Paul. Paul, 'seeing that he had faith to be healed, said with a loud voice, "Stand up straight on your feet!"'—and he was healed, instantaneously, and 'leaped and walked' (vv. 9–10). And the crowd went wild! They shouted in the Lycaonian language, 'The gods have come down to us in the likeness of men!' (v. 11).

Now this extraordinary idea was not unusual in the Greek world. There was actually a legend that Zeus and Hermes had visited this area before, and had only been recognized by one old couple. The people would not want to repeat the mistake!

The irony is that it is not so very far from the truth—that God *has* come down to earth in a human form in Christ, and that Paul and Barnabas were his representatives. The Spirit of Christ was within them and had given them power to heal this man.

But the crowds did more than just proclaim them to be gods. They allocated names to them: 'Barnabas they called Zeus, and Paul, Hermes, because he was the chief speaker' (v. 12).

Zeus was the father of the Greek gods, the Greek equivalent of Jupiter; Hermes was the messenger, the Greek equivalent of Mercury. In ancient statues, Zeus always appears as a father-figure—big, strong and bearded. Hermes is depicted as an athletic young man, ceaselessly active, rushing around with messages from heaven. If only they had known it, Paul was the true messenger, not from Mount Olympus, but from the true God!

But the crowds went further even than that. They next attempted to worship them. 'The priest of Zeus, whose temple was in front of their city, brought oxen and garlands to the gates, intending to sacrifice with the multitudes' (v. 13). It was all very logical. If Paul and Barnabas were gods, then obviously they must worship them!

The whole scene is slightly comic—but Paul and Barnabas are not laughing. On the contrary, 'When the apostles Barnabas and Paul heard this, they tore their clothes and ran in among the multitude, crying out and saying, "Men, why are you doing these things? We also are men with the same nature as you"' (v. 15). They may not have understood at first, not knowing Lycaonian (Greek was the lingua franca of the Empire)—but once they did, they immediately took steps to stop them.

They then began to preach the gospel to them:

We ... preach to you that you should turn from these useless things to the living God, who made the heaven, the earth, the sea, and all things that are in them, who in bygone generations allowed all nations to walk in their own ways. Nevertheless he did not leave himself without witness, in that he did good, gave us rain from heaven and fruitful seasons, filling our hearts with food and gladness (vv. 15–17).

No doubt they would have gone on to speak about Jesus, but it was impossible to continue: 'With these sayings they could scarcely restrain the multitudes from sacrificing to them'.

I quote these words at length, because Luke says *they* spoke them. Luke writes from Paul's perspective, and frequently quotes Paul; he never quotes what Barnabas said—except perhaps here. Maybe Paul was 'the chief speaker', but Barnabas did speak as well!

It is interesting also to notice that Barnabas is called an 'apostle'. The word apostle is sometimes used exclusively of 'the twelve', and sometimes more generally of all who are sent out by the Lord. Barnabas, obviously, was sent out by the Lord just as much as Paul was. Indeed, you may have noticed that he is restored here to first place—'the apostles Barnabas and Paul'—perhaps seeing them through Lycaonian eyes!

Now this adulation by the crowd was in some respects an even greater trial than persecution. What a temptation it must have been!

There is a short story by Rudyard Kipling, *The Man who would be*

King (made into a film in 1975, starring Michael Caine and Sean Connery), in which two soldiers set out to become kings in 'Kafiristan'. They are mistaken for gods, and happily enjoy a life of luxury and worship. But eventually they are found out. One is horribly killed, the other only just escapes to tell the tale. That could have been the story of Paul and Barnabas, had they been less spiritual.

For Barnabas, it was a double temptation—not only to be hailed as a god, but also to be regarded as superior to Paul, having for so long now been number two. He did not give in to the temptation.

But they were nearly killed anyway, because the mood soon changed. 'Then Jews from Antioch and Iconium came there; and having persuaded the multitudes, they stoned Paul and dragged him out of the city, supposing him to be dead' (v. 19). He was not. The disciples gathered round, he rose up and went back into the city.

Do we not hear in all this an echo of the Lord Jesus? He was worshipped by the crowd as he entered Jerusalem, but then the leaders of the Jews 'persuaded the multitudes', and soon they were shouting, 'Crucify him!' He too suffered outside the city, and was left for dead—indeed he *was* dead—but he literally rose again. Like Master, like servant.

The next day they went on to Derbe, preached and won many disciples; that was the limit of this first missionary journey.

It is time to look back and reflect on all this.

FELLOW-SERVANTS

Throughout this journey, Paul and Barnabas are seen as fellow-servants. They work together. True, Paul is 'the chief speaker' and takes the lead—but Barnabas is always with him. Often they are described as acting together, sometimes even speaking together. I do not suppose they spoke in unison, but the words of one were the words of both. We do not even read of them preaching separately in different synagogues. That might have seemed more practical, to get through the region more quickly. Paul could have 'done' Antioch while Barnabas 'did' Iconium. But no—they needed each other, for moral support and mutual prayer.

Our Lord himself set the pattern in Luke 10, when he sent out 'the seventy' (or 'the seventy-two', depending on the manuscript!) 'two by two'. In such dangerous and demanding situations it was wise to go out in twos.

Working together was also implied in their call: 'Separate to me Barnabas and Saul for the work to which I have called them' (13:2). It was a joint work, not an individual work. Even Paul was not a 'Lone Ranger' Christian—he needed Barnabas!

The same principle applies today. There are situations when we must work alone, but in many situations, 'two are better than one, because they have a good reward for their labour. For if they fall, one will lift up his companion' (Ecclesiastes 4:10). When two Christians are working together, often one will lead, and the other support; Barnabas teaches us to take the secondary role graciously. Without Barnabas, Paul could not have achieved what he did.

You can apply this to any area of church life. In youth work, it is wise, for child protection reasons, to have at least two workers (including, usually, at least one female)—but it can also be helpful spiritually. In door-to-door work, some prefer to go alone, because two can be intimidating, and can be mistaken for Jehovah's Witnesses (who normally go out in pairs as well)—but if you have the right partner, one can pray (silently!) while the other speaks, and can step in when the conversation gets difficult. Some pastors could do with a Barnabas to stand alongside them. I thank the Lord for faithful elders who stand alongside me at Lincoln. Even in pastoral visiting, I have found, in many situations, that it is helpful to have my wife visit with me. Sometimes, when we are visiting the ladies, it is even right for her to be 'the chief speaker'!

This is fellowship in service. We use the word 'fellowship' a lot nowadays; we talk about 'fellowship meals' or 'having fellowship over a cup of tea after the service'—and that is good. But fellowship goes beyond being together and talking together. We must learn, like Paul and Barnabas, to *serve* together also.

THE SERVANT IS NOT ABOVE HIS MASTER

Paul and Barnabas repeatedly faced persecution. They would not have been surprised at that. Our Lord himself said in Matthew 10:24–25, 'A disciple is not above his teacher, nor a servant above his master ... If they have called the master of the house Beelzebub, how much more will they call those of his household!' And again, in John 15:18–20, 'If the world hates you, you know that it hated me before it hated you ... Remember the word that I said to you, "A servant is not greater than his master." If they persecuted me, they will also persecute you.'

Persecution can range from mild insults to mortal injury, but it is persecution just the same. We should expect it; we should even rejoice in it. 'Blessed are those who are persecuted for righteousness' sake, for theirs is the kingdom of heaven. Blessed are you when they revile and persecute you, and say all kinds of evil against you falsely for my sake. Rejoice and be exceedingly glad, for great is your reward in heaven, for so they persecuted the prophets who were before you' (Matthew 5:10–12).

Paul and Barnabas were 'filled with joy' when they were persecuted in Antioch (Acts 13:52). To the world, that is incomprehensible; but may the Lord give us the same spirit.

THE SERVANT MUST NOT REPLACE HIS MASTER

I do not imagine that any of us have ever been mistaken for gods, like Paul and Barnabas (though it does happen occasionally in missionary work!). But we do have to face a similar temptation when we are praised by men—perhaps even by our fellow-Christians. We need not be hyper-spiritual and refuse to accept praise—praise should be given where praise is due—but we must beware lest it goes to our heads.

It is possible, sometimes, for a young Christian to idolize an older Christian—perhaps the minister, or the person who led him or her to the Lord, or some father-figure (or mother-figure) who has helped him or her in a special way. Their word becomes law; their example is decisive; in the eyes of the disciple, the master can do no wrong. Very easily, admiration effectively turns into worship (though we would be horrified to think of it that way), and a man or woman has become a god.

It is said that when the Roman emperors rode through the city in triumph, they would have a slave sit in the chariot with them, to whisper in their ear, 'You are only a man'. Yet some of them declared themselves gods all the same! They preferred the roar of the crowd to the whispered truth!

In the world today, pop stars, sports stars, politicians and other celebrities are often treated like gods. Not only is this wrong in the eyes of God—horribly wrong, and liable to the punishment of God ('You shall have no other gods before me', Exodus 20:3)—but it is also spiritually harmful, both to the worshipped and to the worshipper. It is also short-lived—the crowd will always turn eventually.

Herod accepted the worship of the people of Tyre and Sidon, and the Lord struck him down—he was eaten with worms and died, 'because he did not give glory to God' (Acts 12:23). 'I am the LORD, that is my name; and my glory I will not give to another' (Isaiah 42:8).

Paul and Barnabas resisted the temptation; and so must we: 'Not unto us, O LORD, not unto us, but to your name give glory' (Psalm 115:1).

Encouraging the churches

Acts 14:21–28

The return journey from Derbe back to Antioch is covered in just eight verses in Scripture, but there is much here of interest to us. Paul and Barnabas were retracing their step. They encouraged the disciples in the various towns; appointed elders; preached in Perga; and then reported back to their home church in Antioch. Barnabas was involved all along the way.

Encouraging the disciples

First we find them encouraging the disciples: 'They returned to Lystra, Iconium, and Antioch, strengthening the souls of the disciples, exhorting them to continue in the faith, and saying, "We must through many tribulations enter the kingdom of God"' (vv. 21–22).

Barnabas must have been in his element here! As the 'Son of Encouragement' this was precisely the ministry he excelled in. In Acts 11, he had encouraged the new converts in Antioch to continue with the Lord; together with Paul, he did the same here.

It is not difficult to understand why the disciples needed encouragement.

Apart from the difficulties that all new converts face—'the world, the flesh and the devil'—these disciples probably also had to face persecution. Paul and Barnabas themselves had encountered opposition in all these cities; it is unlikely that the opposition would cease after they had left.

Imagine what this might mean. For years you had been going along steadily, attending the local synagogue if you were a Jew, or worshipping Zeus if you were a Greek. Then two strangers had come into town, and turned your world upside down. They had preached about Jesus, the Saviour of the world, and, along with others, you believed in him; now you have joined a little company of believers, meeting every Lord's Day to worship Christ and to study God's Word.

But not everyone feels the same way. There are arguments in the synagogue about it, and you are no longer welcome there. To the Jews, this Jesus is a blasphemer, and Paul and Barnabas mere troublemakers. They regard your conversion as a huge mistake—or worse, a betrayal of all you once stood for.

Or, if you are a Greek, there are the pagan priests to contend with. You can imagine what the priests might say. 'Why don't you go to the Temple of Zeus any more? Why don't you offer up the sacrifices? Surely you know that your failure to sacrifice to Zeus could bring the wrath of the gods upon our city? Surely you are not taken in by those two Jews? Yes, we thought they were gods at first—how embarrassing!—but we soon saw through them!'

There might be quarrels within families, quarrels among friends—just as there are today! People shake their heads as you go off to your little meeting. 'Don't know what you see in it all … What do they get up to in that meeting, anyway?'

Life was very difficult for these new converts.

What a welcome sight it must have been when Paul and Barnabas returned!

For one thing, you might have had just a few niggling doubts. 'They came and preached to us—and then, when the going got tough, they went off and left us!' You might also have questions to ask. Or you might just feel a bit downhearted. It was exciting at first—but now it is just hard work. You would need a word of encouragement.

Paul and Barnabas encouraged these believers in three ways.

Firstly, they 'strengthened' them—no doubt teaching them more fully from the Word of God. Secondly, they 'exhorted them to continue in the faith' and not to give up or go back to Judaism or paganism. Thirdly, they told them the truth about the Christian life—'We must through many tribulations enter the kingdom of God' (v. 22).

Both Paul and Barnabas preached these things—throughout this passage, notice the word 'they'. It was not just Paul.

They themselves were examples to the flock. They had gone through hardships; they had remained true to the faith; they had the moral right to say these things.

They were honest about the difficulties. They did not come to them with glowing promises of health and happiness. They gave it to them straight—they *would* suffer, but afterwards, they would inherit the kingdom of God.

Years later, Paul reflected on this in his letter to Timothy (who came from Lystra), 'But you have carefully followed my doctrine, manner of life, purpose, faith, longsuffering, love, perseverance, persecutions, afflictions, which happened to me at Antioch, at Iconium, at Lystra— what persecutions I endured. And out of them all the Lord delivered me. Yes, and all who desire to live godly in Christ Jesus will suffer persecution' (2 Timothy 3:10–12).

What Paul says of himself could equally have been said about Barnabas.

Appointing elders

They also 'appointed elders in every church' (v. 23).

Presumably when these churches were first founded, no elders were appointed. There may have been no time, or it may not yet have been clear who should be appointed. But now, on their return visit, Paul and Barnabas—together—attend to this matter.

Now these elders could only have been Christians a short while—it was only a few months since Paul and Barnabas had first preached in these cities. We might feel, therefore, that Paul was breaking his own rule, 'not a novice' (1 Timothy 3:6). The churches, however, could not be left leaderless.

No doubt Paul and Barnabas took great care in choosing these elders, looking for men who were 'blameless, the husband of one wife, temperate, sober-minded, of good behaviour, hospitable, able to teach; not given to wine, not violent, not greedy for money, but gentle, not quarrelsome, not covetous ... who rules his own house well, having his children in submission with all reverence ... [having] a good testimony among those who are outside' (1 Timothy 3:2–7).

Barnabas, as we have seen, was a good judge of potential—he had spotted the potential in Paul; no doubt he could judge which of these new converts might prove suitable for the eldership.

Certainly they took it very seriously, with prayer and fasting.

It was not enough for Paul and Barnabas simply to preach the gospel, or even simply to *start* churches. They wanted to *plant* churches—churches that would last, churches that would flourish—and that required elders.

Having appointed elders, they 'commended them to the Lord in whom they had believed', and departed. They were on their way home.

Home at last

Luke mentions that they preached in Perga (v. 25); they had passed through Perga before (13:13), but there is no mention of them preaching at that time. Perga had unhappy memories for them, because it was there that John Mark had left them, but it could not be left out; it was a major town, and it needed the gospel.

Finally, they sailed back from Attalia to Antioch, 'where they had been commended to the grace of God for the work which they had completed' (v. 26). The whole journey had probably taken about a year.

It was time now to report back to the church. 'When they had come and gathered the church together, they reported all that God had done with them, and that he had opened the door of faith to the Gentiles' (v. 27).

How excited the church must have been, and how delighted to hear that the mission had been a success! Having sent out Paul and Barnabas, they were, in a sense, part of the mission—it was 'their' mission, not just Paul and Barnabas' mission. It may be that they had helped to finance it—those long sea voyages had to be paid for, probably in advance, and Paul and Barnabas had not stopped anywhere long enough to earn their own living. Certainly they must have supported them in prayer. How thrilled they must have been to see them back, safe and sound, with such a wonderful story to tell!

Having encouraged the new churches in Lystra, Iconium and Pisidian Antioch, now Paul and Barnabas were encouraging the old church in Syrian Antioch as well.

Every missionary report should refresh our souls. 'As cold water to a weary soul, so is good news from a far country' (Proverbs 25:25).

Afterwards, 'they stayed there a long time with the disciples' (v. 28). They had no further directions from the Lord for the time being, so it was right that they should remain in Antioch, and no doubt continue with their teaching ministry there.

Now as we read all this, perhaps for some there is a sense of nostalgia—'If only it were like that now'. We can make it more like it was, however, if we will learn the art of encouragement.

CHURCHES NEED ENCOURAGEMENT

Many churches are discouraged nowadays—at least in the UK. Some are dwindling in size, and are not seeing conversions in the way they used to; others may be growing, but still feel the strain of living in a 'post-Christian' society. Sometimes we see Christians giving up, or giving in to worldly temptations.

Elsewhere in the world, it may be different. In some lands there is revival. But in many lands, there is the added strain of persecution.

How we need encouragement!

Hebrews 10:24–25 urges us to 'consider one another in order to stir up love and good works, not forsaking the assembling of ourselves together, as is the manner of some, but exhorting one another, and so much the more as you see the Day approaching'. That is what Paul and Barnabas were doing; we must do the same.

We do not know, of course, all that they said, but as far as we know, they did not criticize the churches. They warned them faithfully about the hardships to come, but they did not belittle them, or suggest that they had failed; rather they exhorted them to *continue* in the faith. How we need such a ministry today!

Too often, in the face of difficulty, we panic; we look for changes that will improve the situation.

Sometimes change is necessary; the church that is not open to change is claiming to be perfect—and that is a dangerous claim to make! The Holy Spirit is constantly calling us back from false paths, and redirecting us into the true path; the church that is not open to change, therefore, is not open to the Holy Spirit! But often, the need is simply to *continue*—not to lose our nerve, but to have confidence in our Lord, and in 'the faith which was once for all delivered to the saints' (Jude 3).

LEADERS NEED ENCOURAGEMENT

Paul and Barnabas appointed elders in every church because they saw leadership as important. Yes, the churches could exist without elders—they had existed without elders for some while—but how much better they would function with elders!

Church leaders today have an important and difficult role, and they need encouragement from within the church and from outside. They need to know that they are appreciated, and that people are praying for them, both within the local church, and in other churches.

Some churches, of course, need to be encouraged to appoint leaders. There are many churches trying to survive without pastors. The deacons are doing a heroic job, keeping the church running, often on top of a secular job—but there are many tasks that cannot be done. Some churches are run by a single deacon, or by a single family, who have effectively turned it into a private chapel; others are a free-for-all, where everyone does what is right in his own eyes, without any proper co-ordination or direction.

We cannot simply step in and appoint elders. Paul and Barnabas had apostolic authority. We can only encourage churches to do what is right—and, in the meantime, show appreciation for those who are 'holding the fort'.

MISSIONARIES NEED ENCOURAGEMENT

When they shared what God was doing, Paul and Barnabas were no doubt seeking firstly to glorify God, and secondly to encourage the church. But they too would have been encouraged by the interest shown as the church listened to their report.

Sad to say, not all churches are thrilled to hear missionary reports! It is not that they are not interested in mission. They support mission, financially and in prayer—but all too often, half-heartedly.

Churches that have sent out missionaries will naturally want to hear about 'their' missionary—but what about the wider work? 'All the world is my parish,' Wesley said—and missionary work anywhere in the world ought to excite us.

And what about local missionary work? Do we regularly hear from the Sunday School teachers, about how their work is going? Or the local university Christian Union? Or the Ladies' Meeting? This is not 'their' work, remember—it is 'our' work, the work of the church; we should be encouraging them, and praying for them.

Barnabas was the great encourager—but he too would have needed encouraging sometimes. I am sure that the church at Antioch encouraged him and Paul, on their return. Let us learn to encourage one another in the work!

Resolving conflict

Acts 15:1–35

S atan has many ways of attacking the church. In Antioch and Iconium he used persecution; in Lystra he used flattery. In Acts 15 another danger emerges—false teaching. It is, in fact, a particularly pernicious form of false teaching—falsehood that has an appearance of spirituality.

The circumcision heresy

The point at issue was circumcision. 'Certain men came down from Judea [to Antioch] and taught the brethren, "Unless you are circumcised according to the custom of Moses, you cannot be saved"' (15:1).

To us today, perhaps, this is obviously wrong—but it was not so obvious then. Christianity had its roots in Judaism; the first Christians were Jews. Indeed, to many, Christianity was simply a sect of Judaism. Just as there are Jews today who believe the late Rabbi Schneerson to have been the Messiah, so in the 1st century many people would have regarded Christians as simply a Jewish sect that believed Rabbi Yeshua was the Messiah. As Jews, naturally, they would keep the Law of Moses—and they would expect any Gentile converts to do likewise.

This, after all, was what was expected of converts to Judaism. Many Gentiles were attracted to Judaism, with its one God and its high morals. Some became 'proselytes of the gate' and attended the synagogue without being circumcised—that is how so many Gentiles heard the gospel when Paul and Barnabas preached in the synagogues. But others went the whole way and became converts to Judaism; if they were men, they were circumcised

If Christianity was simply a sect of Judaism, then conversion to Christianity must also require circumcision.

That was the logic of these men from Judea. They were 'zealous for the law', anxious to uphold the ancient traditions, concerned about slipping standards.

Very likely they belonged to the 'sect of the Pharisees' mentioned in verse 5. The Pharisees believed that it was necessary to keep the whole Law in order to be saved; circumcision was therefore necessary. Indeed, they would read in Genesis 17:14, 'And the uncircumcised male child, who is not circumcised in the flesh ... shall be cut off from his people; he has broken my covenant.' To them, this was not just a trivial question of religious rituals or local customs—this was the very heart of their faith.

Paul and Barnabas, however, saw it differently.

Paul himself had been a Pharisee; but his views had changed radically, ever since that encounter on the road to Damascus. As a Levite, Barnabas, too, must have thought about it deeply—and he also had come to a different view.

They themselves, of course, had been circumcised as Jews, but they had never required any of their Gentile converts to be circumcised (though later, Paul circumcised Timothy, probably to avoid needless difficulties when preaching in the synagogues).

Paul explains his reasoning at length in Romans 4 and in Galatians. Essentially, he says, salvation is by faith and not works, and therefore no ritual can possibly be required for salvation.

Thus, for example, in Galatians 3:6 he tackles head-on the

Pharisees' appeal to Abraham: 'Abraham "believed God, and it was accounted to him for righteousness" [quoting Genesis 15:6, which comes, significantly, *before* the passage quoted above, Genesis 17:14]. Therefore know that only those who are of faith are sons of Abraham. And the Scripture, foreseeing that God would justify the Gentiles by faith, preached the gospel to Abraham beforehand, saying "In you all the nations shall be blessed." So then those who are of faith are blessed with believing Abraham.' He challenges those who are circumcised, that they are a 'debtor to keep the whole law' (Galatians 5:3) and no one can do that. Rather, 'Christ has redeemed us from the curse of the law' by dying for us (Galatians 3:13). Now 'in Christ Jesus neither circumcision nor uncircumcision avails anything, but faith working through love' (Galatians 5:6).

Barnabas, evidently, agreed with all this, and together they had put these radical new views into practice, by accepting and baptizing uncircumcised Gentiles who believed in Christ.

Clearly, they were on a collision course with these 'men … from Judea': 'Paul and Barnabas had no small dissension and dispute with them' (15:2). The NIV describes it as a 'sharp dispute'.

Barnabas, 'Mr Valiant-for-Truth'

Now Paul we can understand. Paul comes across as a man very willing to enter into a dispute. He is always gracious, of course, but he is willing to stand up and fight for the truth. Indeed, this particular conflict may have had an extra edge for Paul, because some of these men he probably knew from his days as a Pharisee.

But Barnabas? Is this the same Barnabas we have come to know and love, the 'Son of Encouragement' who is always so gentle and kind? Can we imagine him now, engaged in a 'sharp dispute' over doctrine?

Yet that is what it says—Paul *and* Barnabas were brought into sharp dispute with these men from Judea.

We must recognize here another side to Barnabas' character—a necessary counterbalance. We sometimes imagine that argument and encouragement are mutually exclusive, but that is simply not so. Barnabas cared about doctrine as much as Paul—and he cared about doctrine, because he cared about souls.

This was no trivial issue for Barnabas, any more than it was for the Pharisees. If it were, he might have given way for the sake of peace— but this was a question of salvation.

If it were necessary for Gentile converts to be circumcised as well as believing in Christ, then the death of Christ was insufficient. In that case, his entire gospel was undermined—and hundreds of believers throughout the eastern Mediterranean were unsaved.

One can imagine the argument: Scriptures being quoted and counter-quoted, scrolls unrolled, tempers raised, accusations flying.

These men of Judea would regard Paul as a traitor and Barnabas as a disgrace to his tribe; while Paul and Barnabas would remind them that the Pharisees had always opposed Christ and his gospel.

Nor was it only a private dispute. These men were teaching openly, and some of the Christians in Antioch, no doubt, were convinced by them. Heresy was spreading.

The Jerusalem Council

It was not possible in the end to resolve this conflict locally.

Paul and Barnabas had done the right thing by debating it personally with the men, but they were not convinced, and the church itself was not sure what to believe. Therefore it was necessary to take the matter higher: 'So Paul and Barnabas were appointed, along with some other believers, to go up to Jerusalem to see the apostles and elders about this question' (15:2, NIV).

Paul and Barnabas must have been used by now to being 'sent' on missions like this. Barnabas had been sent to Antioch in 11:22; Paul and Barnabas had been sent to Jerusalem in 11:30; they had been sent out into mission in 13:3; now they are being sent back to Jerusalem to resolve a doctrinal conflict.

There have been many discussions about the status of the meeting that followed in Jerusalem. It is often called 'the Council of Jerusalem', and many see it as the first of many church councils down through the centuries. It is often seen as an example of the local church appealing to a central authority, or at least of one church appealing to another church.

We can certainly draw principles from Acts 15 about church government. At the very least, it shows us that the local church (Antioch) cannot always solve all its problems without outside help. But the truth is that this meeting was unique. The church at Jerusalem was no ordinary church—these were 'the apostles and elders'.

Paul and Barnabas had met these men before. Barnabas had been a member of the church at Jerusalem, and was highly regarded there. Many years earlier, he had brought the proceeds of the sale of his land to the feet of these same apostles; he had also persuaded them to accept Paul. Together they had brought the gifts from Antioch to the church, and Paul at that time had talked with the apostles. Paul himself, at an earlier stage in his life, had lived in Jerusalem. For both men, therefore, this was a homecoming.

Their journey up to Jerusalem was a joyful one. 'Being sent on their way by the church, they passed through Phoenicia and Samaria, describing the conversion of the Gentiles'. They were still bubbling over with all that had happened. And 'they caused great joy to all the brethren' (v. 3).

They were well received in Jerusalem also: 'When they had come to Jerusalem, they were received by the church and the apostles and the elders; and they reported all things that God had done with them' (v. 4). If Galatians 2 refers to this visit, they received at this time the right hand of fellowship, Paul's ministry to the Gentiles being recognized.

But not everyone agreed with them about circumcision. 'Some of the sect of the Pharisees who believed rose up', presumably in a church meeting, and said, 'It is necessary to circumcise them, and to command them to keep the Law of Moses' (v. 5).

It all seems to have been done in a very civilized way. The objection was raised, and 'the apostles and elders came together to consider this matter'. This is not the place to discuss their deliberations in detail—our interest is in Barnabas; but we may just note the sequence of events.

Firstly, there is 'much dispute'—which apparently leads nowhere. Then Peter addressed them, reminding them of the conversion of Cornelius: of how, on that occasion, God had poured out his Spirit upon uncircumcised Gentiles, showing that he accepted them. 'Now therefore, why do you test God by putting a yoke on the neck of the disciples which neither our fathers nor we were able to bear? But we believe that through the grace of the Lord Jesus Christ we shall be saved in the same manner as they' (vv. 10–11). Quite clearly, he agreed with Paul and Barnabas.

The whole assembly now fell silent, and listened to Barnabas and Paul (notice the original order again!) 'declaring how many miracles and wonders God had worked through them among the Gentiles' (v. 12).

Everyone now has had their say. Apostolic authority has spoken; experience has spoken; signs and wonders have spoken.

But how will the matter be decided? By Scripture! After they had become silent, James answered,

Men and brethren, listen to me: Simon has declared to us how God at the first visited the Gentiles to take out of them a people for his name. And with this the words of the prophets agree, just as it is written: 'After this I will return and will rebuild the tabernacle of David which has fallen down; I will rebuild its ruins, and I will set it up; so that the rest of mankind may seek the LORD, even all the Gentiles who are called by my name, says the LORD who does all these things.' Known to God from eternity are all his works (vv. 13–18, quoting from Amos 9:11–12).

James then gave his judgement, 'that we should not trouble those from among the Gentiles who are turning to God', but merely require them 'to abstain from things polluted by idols, from sexual immorality, from things strangled, and from blood' (vv. 19–20).

James evidently was the president of the assembly; he was the Lord's brother and a very godly man. But he does not decide by his own authority, or by what others have said; he is not even persuaded by signs and wonders—but by the Word of God.

Some might feel that the final decision was a bit of a compromise, but it merely required sensitivity over Jewish feelings. There was no compromise over doctrine. Circumcision was not required; justification by faith was effectively upheld.

James' proposal was universally accepted. 'It pleased the apostles and elders, with the whole church, to send chosen men of their own company to Antioch with Paul and Barnabas'—they chose Judas Barsabas and Silas. The letter was written, and the men were sent off and 'came to Antioch; and when they had gathered the multitude together, they delivered the letter' (vv. 22–30). It was accepted at Antioch also: 'When they had read it, they rejoiced over its encouragement' (v. 31). Paul and Barnabas had been vindicated.

Judas and Silas stayed for a while. Being prophets, they 'exhorted and strengthened the brethren with many words'—here were men after Barnabas' own heart! They were then sent back with greetings from the church, but Silas chose to remain (v. 34 NKJV—the NIV omits this verse). Paul and Barnabas also remained, teaching and preaching—as they had before—along with many others (v. 35).

What a joyful time that must have been! Peace was restored!

Now the issue of circumcision has long since been settled (except perhaps in some Messianic fellowships, where the related issue of whether Jews should continue keeping Jewish rituals is still hotly debated). But many other issues have arisen, and still do arise, to this day. Read through any issue of *Evangelical Times*, *Evangelicals Now*, or any other Christian journal, and you will find discussion of the latest heresies. Often they are old heresies dressed up in new clothes; sometimes they appear to be new. The devil is very imaginative in distorting the truth. How do we deal with this? What, in particular, does Barnabas teach us?

TRUTH MATTERS

How easy it would have been for Barnabas to leave it to Paul to debate this issue. Paul was the theologian; he was temperamentally better suited for the task; he knew these men. Leave it to Paul! I will just get on with my ministry of encouraging the brethren. Someone else will sort it out.

But no, Barnabas gets involved—because truth matters to him.

Chapter 8

Truth matters in itself because God is true. Our Lord Jesus Christ is 'the way, the truth, and the life' (John 14:6); he is 'Faithful and True' (Revelation 19:11). To dismiss truth as unimportant is to dismiss Christ as unimportant. Every true Christian is a lover of truth.

But also, truth matters because the eternal salvation of millions depends on it. We find it strange, perhaps, that Barnabas and Paul should quarrel over a Jewish ritual; we find it strange that the bishops at Nicea should quarrel over a single letter in the Creed (*homousia/homoousia*—'of similar substance' or 'of one substance')—but these men understood how so much could depend on apparently so little.

We need to discern, of course, what really matters. There are issues that are trivial. Paul deals with that in Romans 14. But there are also issues that matter, and on these there must be no compromise.

I have been saddened, often, by the lack of interest in doctrinal issues—indeed, sometimes, the hostility to such issues—in Christian circles, and by the willingness of churches to stretch doctrine to embrace everyone. No one, it seems, must ever be told that they are simply wrong! Increasingly, 'anything goes'. I remember being shocked in the 1970s when a leading member of the local Anglican church told me how relieved he was that he didn't have to believe the Creed, because he had difficulty with the virgin birth and the deity of Christ. Those were the days of the famous Bishop of Durham who denied the resurrection. Nowadays, we are pleasantly surprised when a bishop admits he does believe these things!

Doctrine matters. It is the skeleton that holds the Christian together. It is true that, by itself, doctrine is unattractive—a skeleton by itself is dead. But without a skeleton, the body will fall apart. The church needs doctrine.

We must all, like Barnabas, stand firm for the truth.

TRUTH IS NOT IN CONFLICT WITH LOVE

We sometimes fear that, if we insist on the truth, we will appear unloving. We are right to be concerned. But Barnabas shows us that truth and love are not incompatible. Here is one of the most loving of all New Testament characters boldly standing for the truth.

Indeed, how could it be otherwise? The same God who is Truth is also Love. Paul says we must 'speak the truth in love' (Ephesians 4:15). That is precisely what Barnabas was doing.

TRUTH WILL PREVAIL

When this issue first arose, Barnabas and Paul could easily have felt discouraged. They had used their best arguments, and these men of Judea were not convinced. The heresy was spreading; who knew where it might end? When they went up to Jerusalem, they could not be sure how the decision would go. There were many believers of the 'sect of the Pharisees' in Jerusalem, and they were renowned for their holiness. Who knows how much influence they might have over the apostles and elders! James himself had a high reputation with the Jews; he would not want to endanger it. What if they decided against them? Would they have to eat humble pie and go back through all the churches, admitting they were wrong, and circumcise everyone? Would the Gentile believers accept this? Would they break away into splinter churches—'Pro-circumcision' and 'Anti-circumcision' congregations? Would they give up altogether, on the grounds that these Christians didn't know what they believed? What would the world think anyway, seeing this argument?

These were all natural questions—but as far as we can tell,

Barnabas and Paul did not become downcast. They had confidence that the God of truth would uphold his Word. And he did.

Likewise, today we are surrounded by all kinds of heresies. Will the church go under? Of course not! Some, sadly, will be corrupted—and we must do all in our power to prevent that. But our Lord has promised, 'I will build my church, and the gates of Hades shall not prevail against it' (Matthew 16:18).

This episode in Acts 15 should encourage us. Here is one conflict that *was* resolved—thanks in no small measure to Barnabas and Paul. May the Lord help us to resolve the doctrinal conflicts in our own day.

An unresolved conflict

Acts 15:36–41

Paul and Barnabas had avoided division in the church over circumcision by arguing for the truth, and submitting to the elders. Who would have thought that they would divide with each other?

And yet that is what happened. And should we really be surprised? After all, even the apostles were human. Derek Wood, in *The Barnabas Factor*, tellingly subtitles his comments on this section 'St Paul and St Barnabas'. Even holy men can behave in an unholy manner at times.

John Mark

The problem was young John Mark. In chapter 13, we were told, without comment or explanation, that John had departed from them in Pamphylia. That desertion now comes back to haunt them.

The quarrel begins when a new journey is proposed. In 15:36 we are told that, 'After some days Paul said to Barnabas, "Let us go back and visit our brethren in every city where we have preached the word of the Lord, and see how they are doing."' There is no mention of any command from the Lord, nor of any special prayer over this, but it was obviously a good idea, and they agreed to go. But they could not agree on whom to take with them. 'Barnabas was determined to take ... John called Mark. But Paul insisted that they should not take with them the one who had departed from them in Pamphylia, and had not gone with them to the work' (vv. 37–38).

No doubt it began as a quiet disagreement; no doubt they talked it through; but very soon it got out of hand. 'Then the contention became so sharp that they parted from one another. And so Barnabas took Mark and sailed to Cyprus; but Paul chose Silas and departed, being commended by the brethren to the grace of God. And he went through Syria and Cilicia, strengthening the churches' (vv. 39–41).

The Greek word translated 'disagreement' here is *paroxysmos*, from which we get our expression, 'a paroxysm of rage'. This conflict exploded, and as far as we know Paul and Barnabas never worked together again.

There is, however, a rather beautiful sequel. Paul later accepted Mark as a valuable co-worker. In Colossians 4:10, and again in Philemon 24, written during his imprisonment in Rome, he sends greetings from Mark. And in his final imprisonment, in 2 Timothy 4:11, he actually writes 'Get Mark and bring him with you, for he is useful to me for ministry'. Mark subsequently proved his worth by writing one of the four Gospels.

What are we to make of Paul's quarrel with Barnabas?

Who was right?

Almost every Christian I know takes Barnabas' side in this quarrel. Barnabas comes across as the more human of the two, the gentler, more gracious, more far-sighted one. Paul's subsequent acceptance of Mark, and Mark's subsequent ministry, would seem to confirm this— that Barnabas was right and Paul was wrong. It is not, however, as simple as that. Both men had a point.

Let me try to put the case firstly from Paul's point of view. This young man, Mark, had failed them once already, and had probably caused them great inconvenience, leaving them 'in the lurch'. Our Lord had said, 'No one, having put his hand to the plough, and looking back, is fit for the kingdom of God' (Luke 9:62). This projected mission was a dangerous one. Their lives had been threatened before in these towns; they probably would be again. If Mark had given up in Pamphylia, when there was no danger, how would he cope with the perils ahead? Paul probably suspected Barnabas of nepotism—favouring Mark simply because he was his cousin. He was not necessarily rejecting Mark—he would find his ministry elsewhere. But this mission was not the place for him. Someone more reliable was needed. Paul certainly had a case!

But Barnabas also had a case. True, John Mark was his cousin, but that surely was an advantage. He presumably *knew* this young man much better than Paul did; he knew what he was capable of. And surely the family connection would make him all the more loyal. Surely he was entitled to a second chance? After all, the Christian gospel is a gospel of second chances. 'The word of the LORD came to Jonah the second time', after he had run away from God's work and been washed up on the shore (Jonah 3:1). Peter had been given a second chance after he had denied the Lord in the high priest's courtyard. Even Paul himself had been given a second chance, when Barnabas called him out of obscurity in Tarsus, to Antioch! Give Mark a second chance, and he will be all the more determined to prove himself; he will have learned from the previous experience; he will have matured since then. Barnabas also had a case!

But neither was able to see it from the other's point of view. Perhaps the personal element inflamed the argument: 'How *could* Barnabas put his own family interests before the mission?'; 'How *could* Paul accuse me of favouritism, after all these years?'

The quarrel explodes, and like Abraham and Lot thousands of years earlier, there is nothing for it but to part.

Paul proceeds with his plans. Commended by the brethren, he and Silas revisit the churches in Asia Minor, and then go on to Philippi and beyond. The Lord is evidently very much with them.

Barnabas also follows his convictions, by taking Mark on a fresh mission to Cyprus. Nothing is said about the church commending them, and nothing is said about their mission—but it would be unfair to conclude that therefore the church (or the Lord) disapproved. It is just that Luke is telling us Paul's story—after all, he was Paul's companion.

There is much to reflect on here.

NO ONE IS PERFECT

Paul and Barnabas were great men—godly men who lived close to God. But 'the best of men are at best but men'.

They were not the only great Christians to quarrel. Think about Luther and Calvin, disagreeing over the Lord's Supper; or Wesley and Whitefield, disagreeing over election. We ought not to be surprised if lesser mortals like ourselves disagree!

Indeed, this quarrel reminds us that even Paul and Barnabas were sinners like us, in need of the cleansing blood of Christ.

IRON SOMETIMES DENTS IRON

It says in Proverbs 27:17, 'As iron sharpens iron, so a man sharpens the countenance of his friend'. That is how it ought to work! But, as many car drivers know, two metal objects colliding can badly dent each other!

This quarrel arose because of a clash of strengths—not weaknesses. Paul's high standard for himself and others, expecting them to endure and suffer for the faith, was his strength. Likewise Barnabas' kindness and willingness to see potential in others was his strength. They should have combined—but somehow they clashed. To maintain the 'iron on iron' analogy, I suppose it is all a question of angle—approaching it the right way!

DIVISION IS NOT THE END OF THE WORLD

Perhaps the most striking lesson is that God can use our mistakes. Paul and Barnabas quarrel; what is the result? Two missions instead of one! Who knows whether Silas would ever have joined Paul if a 'vacancy' had not arisen? Who knows whether Mark would have got a second chance if Barnabas had gone with Paul—or, if he had, could he have worked successfully under Paul? Who knows whether Barnabas and Paul might have had a more serious quarrel later if they had stayed together?

God moves in a mysterious way
His wonders to perform;
He plants his footsteps in the sea
And rides upon the storm.[1]

It is not uncommon, sadly, for churches to divide, and yet sometimes (not always) God can bring good out of these divisions.

My own church was the result of a division (before my time). By all accounts, it was pretty acrimonious—yet the net result has been two flourishing churches. That is not to defend the split—simply to recognize the sovereign grace of God.

Of course, there is not always a happy ending. I know of one division where both 'halves' have now disappeared. We ought never to take division lightly. Paul teaches us in Ephesians 4:3 to 'make every effort to keep the unity of the Spirit through the bond of peace' (NIV). But when every effort fails, don't despair—pray to the Lord, who 'in all things works for the good of those who love him, who have been called according to his purpose' (Romans 8:28, NIV).

Notes

1 **William Cowper,** *God moves in a mysterious way.*

No hard feelings

Galatians 2:1–13; 1 Corinthians 9; Colossians 4:10

Barnabas disappears from Acts after the quarrel in chapter 15; Luke follows Paul on his travels and says no more about Barnabas. There is nothing sinister in that: he says no more about Peter either.

But Barnabas is not forgotten. His name appears several more times in Paul's letters, always in an honourable light.

There were no hard feelings with Paul. He remembers Barnabas with affection; he respects him as a fellow-worker. Whether or not he kept in touch with him, we don't know; it would be nice to think that he prayed for him, and that Barnabas prayed for Paul.

Division does not mean that we have to cut ourselves off for ever, or vilify our former friends. On the contrary, we ought to maintain whatever fellowship is possible, and look for reconciliation.

There are three references to Barnabas, which we will take in their likely chronological order.

Even Barnabas (Galatians 2:1–13)

Galatians takes up the circumcision controversy of Acts 15. Commentators differ, but it seems likely that the visit to Jerusalem described in Galatians 2 is the visit in Acts 15. Paul recalls how, 'After fourteen years I went up again to Jerusalem with Barnabas' and how James, Peter and John, those reputed to be pillars, gave to 'me and Barnabas the right hand of fellowship' (Galatians 2:1,9). The mission to the Gentiles was officially approved.

However, an ugly incident followed. Some time afterwards, there was a further conflict with the circumcision party.

'When Peter had come to Antioch, I withstood him to his face,' Paul writes, 'because he was to be blamed; for before certain men came from James, he would eat with the Gentiles; but when they came, he withdrew and separated himself, fearing those who were of the circumcision. And the rest of the Jews also played the hypocrite with him, so that even Barnabas was carried away with their hypocrisy.'

Hard-line Jews would not eat with the Gentiles, for fear of ritual contamination. That was the complaint against Peter in Acts 11:3: 'You went in to uncircumcised men and ate with them!' The Jerusalem Council had agreed that Gentile believers need not be circumcised, but it had not said that Jews must eat with them!

One can imagine Barnabas looking to Peter for guidance, seeing what the others were doing, and finally declining to eat with the Gentiles.

How shocked Paul must have been! Barnabas, who had seen the grace of God upon the Gentiles in Antioch; Barnabas, who had accompanied him on his missionary journey; Barnabas, who had seen Gentiles converted; Barnabas, who had stood with him at the Jerusalem Council; even Barnabas had now turned traitor to the cause. It may even have contributed to their separation, undermining Paul's trust in Barnabas.

But notice the word 'even'. '*Even* Barnabas was led astray'. That little word 'even' speaks volumes as to the esteem with which Paul held Barnabas, even years later when he wrote Galatians.

Often, when we quarrel with someone, we look back and read bad motives into everything they did. 'I should have seen it coming,' we say, 'he was always a little suspect.' There is nothing of that here. Paul seems to regard Barnabas as even less likely to go astray than Peter. Paul still has a high regard for Barnabas. There are no hard feelings.

Only Barnabas (1 Corinthians 9)

Paul's letter to the Corinthians was probably written from Ephesus about AD 55, during the second missionary journey—long after Paul and Barnabas had separated. And yet he regards him still as a fellow-worker.

In chapter 9, he is defending his apostleship. Questions are being asked as to whether this unassuming man, who had taken lodgings with a married couple in Corinth and worked as a tentmaker (Acts 18:3), and who preached in his spare time, could possibly be an apostle. They expected, perhaps, something grander than that. Paul answers that he had every right to work or not to work, to marry or not to marry. He had chosen to live as he did for the sake of the gospel.

But he includes Barnabas in this: 'My defence to those who examine me is this: Do we have no right to eat and drink? Do we have no right to take along a believing wife, as do also the other apostles, the brothers of the Lord and Cephas? Or is it only Barnabas and I who have no right to refrain from working?' (vv. 3–6).

Now Barnabas had not been with Paul at Corinth; as far as we know, he had never visited Corinth. Why mention him at all? Because Paul still thought of him as a fellow-worker, who had shared his lifestyle. And Paul appreciated that. There were very few who were prepared to make sacrifices for the sake of the gospel. Even the other apostles (who had made huge sacrifices in the past) presumably expected the churches to support them. Only Barnabas had fully shared in Paul's vision, and lived as Paul lived.

Paul still held him in high regard. There were no hard feelings.

The renowned Barnabas (Colossians 4:10)

There is much to be learned from the greetings in Paul's letters. Here in Colossians he sends greetings from prison in Rome: 'Aristarchus my fellow prisoner greets you, with Mark the cousin of Barnabas (about whom you received instructions: if he comes to you, welcome him)'.

This shows, firstly, that Paul was reconciled to Mark. Presumably Mark had visited him in Rome (it is said that he wrote his Gospel there). Paul now recognized the worth of this young man. Later he wrote: 'Get Mark and bring him with you, for he is useful to me for ministry' (2 Timothy 4:11). Barnabas was right!

But it also shows the respect with which Barnabas was regarded, that Mark could be recommended simply as 'the cousin of Barnabas'. In faraway Colosse, they had heard of Barnabas—Barnabas was renowned.

Barnabas in glory

Rather surprisingly, the Bible does not say what happened to Barnabas. But then, we are not told what happened to Paul either.

Later traditions say that he was martyred in Salamis in Cyprus in AD 61; his tomb was allegedly discovered in the 4th century, and a monastery built on the site.

Far more important, we know where Barnabas is now! He is 'with Christ, which is far better' (Philippians 1:23), awaiting the glorious day of the resurrection. 'Blessed are the dead who die in the Lord ... "Yes", says the Spirit, "that they may rest from their labours, and their works follow them"' (Revelation 14:13). That surely is true of Barnabas, the 'Son of Encouragement'.

Barnabas the author?

With as attractive a character as Barnabas, it is natural to wonder whether he wrote anything. After all, Paul did; why not Barnabas?

Several writings have been attributed to him, but there is no real evidence to support any of them. It is important, however, to consider them.

The Epistle to the Hebrews

Tertullian, about AD 200, suggested that Barnabas was the author of the anonymous Epistle to the Hebrews—but this has never gained any widespread acceptance.

The Epistle of Barnabas

This remarkable letter is counted among the writings of the 'Apostolic Fathers'. It is readily available in modern translations (including a Penguin Classic entitled *Early Christian Writings*). Twenty-eight pages long in the Penguin edition, it consists mostly of allegorical interpretations of the Old Testament followed by a short exhortation to godly living. Some of these interpretations are fanciful in the extreme. The writer finds the crucifixion, for example, in Abraham's 318 servants—the Greek letters for 318 being IET: IE are the first two letters of Jesus, and T is for the cross! Likewise the various unclean animals in Leviticus are compared with various kinds of sinners!

It was held in high regard by the early church. Origen refers to the 'Catholic Epistle of Barnabas'; the Codex Sinaiticus, in the British

Museum, has it bound together with the New Testament. Eusebius, however, lists it among books rejected from the canon.

It is a fascinating book—but is it by Barnabas?

The epistle itself is anonymous (like Hebrews!) and the first suggestion that it was by Barnabas came from Clement of Alexandria, towards the end of the 2nd century. Origen and Jerome followed this view, but it seems unlikely. Modern scholars think it was probably written by an Alexandrian Jew about AD 130.

The Acts of Barnabas

This apocryphal work claims to be by Mark, not Barnabas—but in any case it is thought to have been written in the 5th century.

The Gospel of Barnabas

Christians need to be aware of the so-called 'Gospel of Barnabas'. This is frequently cited by Muslims as the 'true gospel'. It begins, 'True Gospel of Jesus, called Christ, a new prophet sent by God to the world: according to the description of Barnabas, his apostle.'[1] You do not have to read far, however, to sense Islamic influence. On the very first page we are warned that 'many are preaching most impious doctrine, calling Jesus son of God ...' Later, Jesus receives a book from Gabriel (rather like Muhammad), and reference is made to Abraham offering Ishmael, not Isaac. Jesus also says, 'After me shall come the Splendour of all the prophets and holy ones, and shall shed light upon the darkness of all that the prophets have said, because he is the messenger of God'. Later he actually names him as Muhammad!

Jesus is not crucified at all in this supposed 'Gospel'. He is rescued by the angels and taken up to the third heaven when Judas comes to betray him; Judas is changed to look like Jesus, and crucified instead!

Jesus then appears again to his disciples. Barnabas (who is presented as one of the disciples) is then commanded to write.

What are we to make of all this?

Scholars believe it is a medieval forgery, written probably in Spain in the 14th century. It contains echoes of Dante, and many medieval ideas completely alien to the 1st century. It was certainly not written by Barnabas!

It would appear, therefore, that we do not have any genuine writings by Barnabas. However, his life is his epistle to us. 'He, being dead, still speaks' (Hebrews 11:4). May we listen to his voice.

Notes

1 The full text can be read at http://www.barnabas.net/barnabasP1.html.

COLIN D JONES

ISBN 978–1–84625–089–7

96PP PAPERBACK

The story of Samson is one of the most exciting and intriguing in the whole of Scripture. As the sub-title suggests, it is a simultaneous insight into his incredible strength and persistent weakness. We marvel at the thrilling accounts of unorthodox battles and awe inspiring demonstrations of physical power. Sadly, we also wonder at his apparent inability to learn from his own mistakes as he follows his passions to their inevitable end. This rollercoaster of a story sweeps us from the rich promises accompanying his birth, though the tragedies and triumphs of his life. The story almost ends with the pitiable sight of him as the blind captive of his life-long enemies the Philistines. Yet, there is still one surprising twist to this epic tale—victory through death. Throughout we trace the contrasts with the great Judge of Israel—Christ.

Colin D Jones has been in the ministry since 1971. He became the pastor of Three Bridges Free Church, Crawley in 1996 after twenty-two years of ministry at Wem Baptist Church, Shropshire. He is a long serving member of the Council of the FIEC and is author of *Exploring Esther: Serving the unseen God*, also published by Day One. He and his wife, Chris, have four daughters: Esther, Abigail, Tirzah and Miriam.

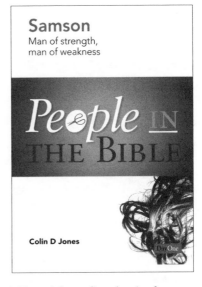

Samson
Man of strength,
man of weakness

People IN
THE BIBLE

Colin D Jones

Read this work for profit and praise, for a greater than Samson has come into the world.
CLIVE ANDERSON, PASTOR OF 'THE BUTTS' CHURCH, ALTON, HAMPSHIRE, ENGLAND

'Colin Jones has made an enigmatic narrative powerfully relevant. This is the story of Samson—for today. Careful exegesis, confronting the hard parts with honesty, and comparing and contrasting with the life of Jesus Christ, together with practical application, makes this commentary a powerful blend of personal Bible Study aid, a group discussion starter and a challenge for every Christian life. An accessible must for anyone interested in the life and times of Samson and its relevance for today.'
BRIAN H EDWARDS